Claws and Order goes Extreme

End Cat Rivalries: Build Trust, Create Harmony, and Enjoy a Peaceful Multi-Cat Home

Chris Williams

Contents

The Feline Social Structure

Alpha, Beta and Omega

Alpha, Beta and Omega

The Alpha Cat: Who's Really in Charge?

This chapter is the foundation for understanding feline social structures, which is key to creating a peaceful and well-balanced home for your cats. By understanding the dynamics between alpha, beta, and omega cats, you can create a more harmonious multi-cat environment, and this understanding will be crucial as we explore further specific behavioural insights throughout this book.

Picture this: you walk into your living room, and there on the couch sits your cat, comfortably sprawled out, eyes half-closed, barely acknowledging your presence. Who's really in charge here? Is it you, the cat owner, or is it actually your feline friend? This section delves into the complex cat social hierarchy and determines who's really in charge—the alpha cat.

The alpha cat in your household is the one who dictates the rules, sets the schedule, and demands the most attention, like a tiny furry dictator. You may think you are making decisions, but watch as your cat gives you that look that says, "I'm in charge here." Whether it's deciding when it's time to be fed or when it's time for cuddles, the alpha cat always has the final say.

But don't worry, being the alpha cat is not all fun and games. Great power comes with great responsibility, and your feline friend takes their role very seriously. They may demand the best spot on the couch or the warmest spot in bed, but at the end of the day, they are just looking out for their well-being and comfort—because nothing less will do for royalty.

The alpha cat is often the first to explore new areas of the house, marking their territory with confidence and ensuring that every corner of their domain is secure. Mieshelle Nagelschneider, a well-known cat behaviourist, explains that alpha cats rely on visual signals and body language to assert dominance without physical aggression (Nagelschneider, 2023). [1] This vigilance and leadership are what keep the household stable and predictable for the rest of the cats. According to Dr Jackson Galaxy, a cat behaviourist, alpha cats use these signals to maintain social order without resorting to aggression (Galaxy, 2023).[2]

When the alpha cat is confident and calm, the rest of the household tends to follow suit. They are often the first to investigate anything new—a new piece of furniture, a new pet, or even a visitor. Their curiosity and courage

---

1. M. Nagelschneider, "The Cat Behavior Clinic: Understanding Alpha Cat Behavior," The Cat Behavior Clinic, 2023

2. J. Galaxy, "Alpha Cats and Their Social Signals," Galaxy's Cat World, 2023.

set an example for the other cats, helping them to feel more comfortable in their environment.

The alpha cat's leadership is about asserting dominance and providing a sense of stability and order that benefits everyone in the household. Understanding these roles not only enriches our appreciation of our feline companions but also equips us with the tools needed to ensure all our cats coexist happily. Their influence extends beyond their feline companions; their behaviour also affects human members of the household. For instance, they often communicate their needs through distinct vocalizations or by using body language to signal what they want.

This kind of assertive behaviour can make the human-cat bond even stronger as cat owners learn to recognize and respond to these cues. Alpha cats have a unique way of training their owners, ensuring that everything is arranged just the way they like it.

So, the next time you find yourself wondering who's really in charge, just look at your cat's confident strut and know that the alpha cat reigns supreme in your household. Embrace your cat's unique personality and appreciate the special bond you share with one of the most majestic creatures in the animal kingdom—your beloved feline. After all, having an alpha cat in your home means you always have a leader to rely on, someone who will protect their territory and ensure that everything runs according to their rules. Their protective instincts and watchful nature are what make them invaluable, and their strong sense of responsibility keeps the household running smoothly. The alpha cat is not just a leader but also a teacher—helping other cats and even their human companions understand the value of order and routine.

Transitions: From Alpha to Beta to Omega

While the alpha cat leads with confidence and demands respect, there are other important roles that help maintain balance in the household. Beta cats support the alpha's leadership by mediating conflicts and ensuring household harmony, while omega cats bring calmness and stability through their adaptable and observant nature. Understanding how these roles interact is key to ensuring harmony in a multi-cat environment. Let's move on to the next role: the beta cat, the essential right-hand companion to the alpha.

Transition to Beta Cats

While the alpha cat takes the lead, beta cats serve as essential support figures who keep the peace and help manage the daily needs of the group. Let's delve into the role of the beta cat.

The Beta Cats: The Right-Hand Cats

In the world of cats, a hierarchy exists as complex and nuanced as any human society. At the top of this feline social ladder are the alpha cats, the fearless leaders who rule with an iron paw. Then there are the beta cats, the loyal followers who act as the right-hand companions to the alphas. These beta cats may not be in charge, but they play a crucial role in maintaining order within the household.

Beta cats are the unsung heroes of the feline world, often doing the hard work while the alpha takes all the credit. For instance, when two cats start a standoff over a favourite spot, the beta cat often moves in to diffuse the tension by distracting one of the cats or calmly taking over the space themselves.

They may not get all the attention or glory that the alphas do, but they are the ones who keep things running smoothly behind the scenes. They mediate disputes between other cats, ensure everyone is fed and groomed, and keep the household peaceful. For example, a beta cat might calm a confrontation by sitting between two agitated cats or encourage harmony by grooming others when tensions are high. In many ways, they are the true power players of the cat world.

Despite the challenges they face, beta cats take their role seriously. They understand that without their steady presence and calming influence, the household would descend into chaos, with constant fights over territory, disrupted routines, and increased stress levels among all the cats.

They may not always get the credit they deserve, but they know their contributions are invaluable in keeping peace and harmony within the feline community. Understanding their patience and nurturing nature helps cat owners provide the best care, ensuring the household remains peaceful. They often act as peacekeepers, stepping in when the alphas are too demanding or when the omega cats feel left out. Their ability to adapt and manage relationships between all the cats makes them invaluable. Dr Sophia Yin, a veterinary behaviourist, also notes that beta cats often engage in calming behaviours such as grooming, which help reinforce social bonds and reduce group tension (Yin, 2023).[3]

For instance, they might initiate a group grooming session, which not only helps with hygiene but also serves as a bonding activity that strengthens the group's social structure. These small yet meaningful actions keep the household from falling apart, and their dedication ensures every cat feels a sense of belonging.

In addition to their peacekeeping duties, beta cats often help maintain order by reinforcing the alpha cat's rules. They understand the hierarchy and work to support the alpha's leadership, which helps create a stable environment. Beta cats are also incredibly empathetic. They can sense when one of the other cats is feeling anxious or stressed, and they often step in to provide comfort, whether it's through grooming, snuggling, or simply sitting close by.

Their nurturing nature helps to diffuse tensions and fosters a sense of community among the cats. Their actions are often subtle, but their effect on the household is profound—helping to establish trust and create a cooperative environment.

Beta cats also play an important role in ensuring that the household runs efficiently. They often take on the enforcer role, ensuring that the more

---

3. Dr. Sophia Yin. "The Role of Beta Cats in Maintaining Feline Harmony," Veterinary Behavior Journal, 2023.

submissive cats follow the established rules. When the alpha cat has set boundaries—like which areas are off-limits or when it's time to eat—the beta cat helps to enforce these boundaries, ensuring that everyone respects the order of the household.

Their loyalty to the alpha and dedication to maintaining harmony make them indispensable members of the feline family. Beta cats often serve as mediators not only for the feline members of the household but also in the human-cat dynamic. They bridge the gap between the often more demanding alpha and the rest of the family, making sure everyone feels at ease. Their calm demeanour helps alleviate stress, especially during times of change, such as introducing a new pet or moving homes. Their flexibility and adaptability allow them to manage different personalities effectively, ensuring the household remains stable.

Tips for Supporting Beta Cats in a Multi-Cat Household

- **Recognize Their Role**: Understand and appreciate the role of the beta cat in keeping peace and maintaining harmony. Acknowledge their contributions by giving them extra affection and positive reinforcement for their calming actions.

- **Encourage Social Bonding**: Facilitate bonding activities like group grooming sessions or interactive play that includes all the cats. Beta cats thrive on social interactions, and encouraging these moments helps strengthen their relationships with other cats.

- **Provide Safe Spaces**: Ensure the beta cat has access to cosy hiding spots or elevated areas where they can retreat if they feel overwhelmed. This is particularly important when tensions are high, as beta cats may need a break from mediating conflicts.

- **Positive Reinforcement**: Reward the beta cat when they successfully diffuse conflicts or exhibit positive behaviour, such as grooming or comforting another cat. This recognition reinforces their role as a peacekeeper. Regular rewards can help strengthen their confidence and maintain their position as an effective mediator.

- **Monitor Stress Levels**: Since beta cats are often the ones managing relationships, it's crucial to keep an eye on their stress levels. Providing mental stimulation with puzzle toys or giving them one-on-one attention can help reduce stress. Incorporating calming elements like pheromone diffusers in the household can also support beta cats in their role, creating a more relaxed environment for everyone.

These tips will help ensure that beta cats receive the support they need to continue their vital role in maintaining household harmony, allowing them to thrive and feel valued in the feline community. By giving beta cats the recognition and support they deserve, you can help foster a peaceful and happy home for all your furry friends.

Transition to Omega Cats

After understanding the alpha and beta cats, we move to another key player—the omega cat. Often misunderstood, omega cats bring unique skills to maintain balance in the household.

The Omega Cat: The Underdog or the Master Manipulator

In the world of feline social hierarchy, there is one cat that often gets overlooked—the omega cat. This underdog of the cat world is often seen as the one who doesn't quite fit in with the rest of the pride. But is the omega cat truly just a lowly member of the pack, or could they quietly influence the dynamics behind the scenes?

Many cat owners may underestimate the omega cat, assuming they are simply the runt of the litter or the cat that always gets picked on by others. In reality, the omega cat may actually be the true mastermind, quietly ruling from the shadows. However, don't be fooled by their seemingly meek demeanour. The omega cat may be calling the shots without you even realizing it. For example, they might quietly take over their favourite nap spot by waiting for just the right moment when the other cats leave it unattended. They have a way of subtly manipulating the other cats in the household to get what they want, whether it's the best spot on the couch or the last bit of tuna in the bowl.

While the alpha cat may be the one who appears to be in charge, it's the omega cat who is often the real power player. They know how to use their charm and cunning to get what they want, all while flying under the radar. For instance, an omega cat might patiently wait for the other cats to get distracted before slipping in to claim the warmest spot in the house with ninja-level patience. So next time you think your omega cat is just a pushover, think again—they may be the true mastermind of the household.

But don't worry, being the omega cat doesn't mean they are any less deserving of love and attention. In fact, many cat owners find that their omega cat is the most lovable and affectionate of the bunch. They may not be the loudest or most assertive, but they can work their way into your heart and make you wonder how you ever lived without them. Whether it's the gentle nudge of their head seeking affection or their habit of curling up next to you at just the right moment, omega cats know how to make themselves irreplaceable. Dr Sarah Ellis, a feline behaviour expert, points out that omega cats' observant nature allows them to respond effectively to household dynamics, preventing potential conflicts (Ellis, 2023).

This keen sense of observation allows them to find opportunities to get what they want without causing conflict. For example, an omega cat might notice when the alpha cat is preoccupied and use that moment to access a coveted spot or resource. Their ability to navigate the social landscape with subtlety and finesse is what makes them so effective at getting their needs met without direct confrontation.

Omega cats also have a knack for maintaining household harmony, often in surprising ways. They might engage in playful antics to diffuse tension, using humour and charm to distract other cats from potential conflicts. Their laid-back approach allows them to become a buffer between the more dominant personalities in the household, promoting a sense of calm and stability.

Omega cats are masters of understanding timing—they instinctively know when to approach another cat or human for affection and when to stay back, which helps keep the overall atmosphere relaxed and peaceful.

So, the next time you see your omega cat lounging in the sun or snuggled up on your lap, remember that they may just be the unsung hero of the household. They may not be the biggest or the boldest, but they are certainly a force to be reckoned with. Embrace your omega cat for their unique ability to influence the household dynamics, and watch as they continue to win over your heart with their quiet charm and endearing ways. Their gentle persistence and lovable quirks make them an irreplaceable part of your feline family. Their ability to observe and adapt often means they know just when to offer comfort, whether during a stressful moment or when you need extra love. The omega cat's quiet strength and unassuming nature are what make them so special, and their presence brings a sense of balance and warmth to your home.

Omega cats also have the remarkable ability to bring a sense of calm to the household, like a feline yoga instructor, promoting inner peace. Unlike alpha cats, which sometimes stir up excitement or tension, omega cats often help maintain a peaceful atmosphere. Their laid-back nature can be infectious, encouraging the other cats to relax and take it easy. This calming influence is especially valuable in a multi-cat household, where conflicts can arise, and tensions can run high. By providing a consistent source of gentle affection and tranquillity, omega cats help to create a harmonious environment where all the cats can coexist peacefully.

Tips for Supporting Omega Cats in a Multi-Cat Household

- **Provide Safe Retreats**: Omega cats need places where they can escape the hustle and bustle of the household. Set up cosy hideaways, such as cat caves, boxes, or soft beds, where they can feel safe and relaxed.

- **Reward Independence**: Omega cats often wait patiently for the right moment to get what they want. Reward their patience with treats or affection to reinforce their behaviour and help them feel valued. Regular rewards can also help boost their confidence, allowing them to engage more actively with other members of the household.

- **Encourage Play**: Even omega cats need playtime to build confidence. Engage them in gentle, interactive play sessions that boost their self-esteem without overwhelming them. This can include using feather toys, softballs, or other gentle activities that allow them to express themselves without feeling intimidated.

- **Monitor Interactions**: Omega cats can sometimes be overshadowed by more dominant cats. Make sure they get enough food, attention, and rest without being pushed aside by the alpha or beta cats. Feeding them in a separate area can help ensure they aren't bullied out of their meals. Monitoring these interactions closely can also help prevent undue stress and ensure the omega cat feels secure.

- **Celebrate Their Role**: Omega cats may not be the loudest or the boldest, but they contribute significantly to household harmony. Celebrate their role by giving them extra cuddles and acknowledging the comfort and peace they bring to the group. Showing appreciation for their calming presence helps them feel like an important part of the family dynamic.

These tips will help omega cats thrive in a multi-cat household, ensuring they feel secure, loved, and an integral part of the family dynamic. Omega cats, with their quiet strength and gentle nature, bring a unique balance to the household that should always be cherished. Their ability to read the room and adapt accordingly is a skill that helps them survive and makes the entire household thrive.

Recap: Understanding Alpha, Beta, and Omega Cats

In this chapter, we explored the unique roles of alpha, beta, and omega cats. Each role is essential to household dynamics: alpha cats lead confidently, beta cats support and mediate, and omega cats bring adaptability and calmness to ensure a peaceful household.

What's Next?

In the next chapter, we'll delve into specific behavioural strategies that can help foster better relationships among your cats and ensure a peaceful multi-cat household. By understanding the foundational roles of alpha, beta, and omega cats, you are now equipped to take a deeper dive into how these dynamics play out in everyday situations.

In summary, understanding the alpha, beta, and omega roles in your household will help you create a nurturing environment that accommodates the unique needs and personalities of each of your feline friends. Recognizing these dynamics is key to ensuring harmony in a multi-cat household.

The Enigmatic World of Feline Emotions

Start to understand your cat

Cats are often seen as aloof and mysterious, but the truth is they have rich emotional lives that many people fail to recognize. Their emotions may not be as obvious as a dog's wagging tail, but if you pay close attention, you'll see how expressive they are. Much like that one coworker who barely speaks but knows everything that's happening in the office, cats quietly observe and feel deeply. They may not wag their tails like dogs or greet you with wet kisses, but their emotions are just as complex—and perhaps even more interesting. Dr Emily Green, a feline behaviour specialist, states, "Understanding cat emotions is key to forming a deeper bond, allowing owners to provide better care and build trust."[1] For example, a rapidly flicking tail can indicate agitation. Giving your cat space when they show this sign can help reduce stress and build a stronger, more trusting

---

1. Dr. Emily Green, "Understanding Cat Behavior and Emotions," Feline Emotional Studies Journal, 2022

relationship. Whether it's the look in their eyes or the subtle twitch of a whisker, every gesture tells a story, and cat owners who pay attention can learn a lot about their furry friends.

Understanding Cat Emotions: It's Not Just About the Purr

Most cat owners are familiar with the classic indicators of a happy cat, such as purring or kneading, but these are just the tip of the iceberg. Cats have a wide range of emotions, from joy and curiosity to fear and irritation. For example, how a cat flicks its tail or positions its ears can say a lot about how it feels. Dr Jane Smith, an animal behaviourist, notes, "Recognizing subtle emotional cues such as ear positioning or tail flicking is crucial for understanding a cat's mood."[2] Set aside some dedicated time each day to quietly observe your cat's behaviour—note how they react to different stimuli and interactions. This simple practice will help you become more attuned to their emotional cues, strengthening your bond. According to Dr. Andrew Johnson, a feline psychologist, "Cats can exhibit jealousy when they see their human giving attention to another pet. This behaviour is typical of animals that form strong attachment bonds."[3] It's like they're saying, "Excuse me, I'm the star here."

Cat in a Stealthy Pose

2. Dr. Jane Smith, "Deciphering Cat Mood Indicators," Animal Behavior Insights, 2023.

3. Dr. Andrew Johnson, "Jealousy in Domestic Cats," Journal of Feline Psychology, 2021.

The challenge lies in the fact that cats are masters of masking their feelings—secret agents of the animal kingdom if you will. For example, a cat may calmly sit by the window as if uninterested, but in reality, they are closely observing their surroundings, ready to react if something catches their attention. Unlike dogs, who are openly expressive, cats have a much more subtle approach to showing their emotions.

A slow blink, for instance, is often a sign of trust and affection—a 'feline kiss,' if you will. On the other hand, a twitching tail is a clear signal of agitation and a cue for you to keep your distance. Cat owners who learn to read these cues will understand their feline friends much more deeply.

It's also fascinating to see how cats use their environment to hide their true emotions—like curling up in high places to feel safe or tucking their tails close to their bodies to appear smaller and less threatening. They're like little ninjas with fur, always strategizing.

Cats are also known for their unique personalities, which means their emotional expressions can vary significantly among individual cats. Some cats are more vocal about their needs, while others are quiet observers who communicate mostly through body language. Understanding these individual quirks can make a world of difference in interpreting their emotional states.

Some cats may chirp or trill with excitement, while others may express joy by playfully pouncing around. Each cat has its own way of saying, 'I'm happy!' Encouraging these behaviours with interactive toys or offering praise during playtime can create a positive environment where your cat's natural expressions of joy can flourish.

Zoomies in Action

And let's not forget the infamous "zoomies"—those bursts of energy where cats race around the house like they've just had an espresso shot. The zoomies often indicate that a cat is feeling particularly joyful or trying to release pent-up energy. Observing and learning these behaviours can foster a stronger connection with your cat, plus it's endlessly entertaining.

Cat Rubbing Against Human Leg

Cats may also show signs of affection by rubbing against you, which is their way of marking you with their scent and claiming you as part of their territory. This behaviour clearly indicates that they consider you part of their trusted circle. In cat terms, you're officially part of the family—lucky you! It's important to remember that each cat has its own personality, and what works to bond with one cat might not work with another. Learning these nuances can make your relationship with your cat much richer.

Signs of Cat Emotions and How to Read Them

Content Cat Relaxing

- **Curiosity and Playfulness**: Curiosity is a big part of a cat's emotional life. Cats express curiosity by perking their ears, dilating their pupils, and focusing intensely on an object or movement. They might engage in playful behaviours, like pouncing or batting at toys, indicating they're energetic and inquisitive. Playfulness is often a way for cats to express their inner hunter, and engaging in these behaviours helps satisfy their natural instincts. Playtime is also an important outlet for pent-up energy, and providing interactive toys can help your cat stay mentally and physically stimulated. Plus, it's great entertainment—who doesn't love watching a cat go full ninja on a feather toy?

- **Fear and Anxiety**: Fear is an emotion that cats may display in various ways, depending on the individual cat. Common signs of fear include flattened ears, dilated pupils, and a crouched posture. A fearful cat may also hide or run away to avoid a perceived threat. Recognizing these signs is important, as addressing the cause of fear can help reduce your cat's anxiety. For instance, providing a safe hiding spot or using a calming pheromone diffuser can make a big difference in helping your cat feel more secure. Fearful cats may also avoid eye contact; some may growl or hiss to communicate discomfort. It's their way of saying, "Back off, I'm not in the mood."

- **Irritation and Aggression**: A cat that feels irritated or aggressive often displays warning signs before lashing out. These can include a swishing tail, flattened ears, hissing, or even a growl. If a cat's pupils are narrowed and its body stiff, it's best to give it space. Knowing when to back off can prevent scratches or bites and help maintain a positive relationship. Cats may also show irritation if they feel overstimulated during petting, so paying attention to their body language can prevent negative interactions. Remember, when a cat's had enough, they've *really* had enough—ignore their warnings at your own peril.

- **Affection and Trust**: Cats show affection differently than other pets. Cats express love and trust by headbutting, rubbing against your legs, or curling up next to you. The famous slow blink is like a feline kiss, indicating comfort and safety around you. Returning a slow blink is a good way to show your cat you care. Cats may also groom their owners as a sign of affection, treating you as part of their family. Grooming is a form of bonding and a way for cats to reinforce their social structure. When a cat grooms you, it shows that it trusts you deeply and considers you part of its social circle—congratulations, you're officially one of the cool cats.

The Complex Emotional Bond Between Cats and Humans

Cats have unique ways of bonding with their human staff; understanding their emotions is a huge part of fostering this bond. Unlike dogs, who are often eager to please, cats prefer relationships that are based on mutual respect— though let's be honest, they're usually the ones setting the terms. They value their independence, but this does not mean they cannot form deep connections.

Cats demonstrate these connections by choosing to be near their favourite humans, sharing routines, and offering comfort during difficult times. Whether it's following you from room to room or simply resting nearby, these small gestures reveal the depth of their attachment. For example, when you move from the kitchen to the living room and your cat follows, settling in a spot where they can watch you, it's their way of showing that they feel connected to you and want to be near you. These moments, though subtle, are powerful indicators of the bond they share with you—and let's face it, they also want to keep an eye on their food provider.

A cat's bond with its owner can be seen in how it chooses to spend time nearby, follow you from room to room (like a furry shadow), or rest in a spot where it can keep an eye on you—because someone has to supervise your activities. These actions show that your cat is emotionally attached to you and trusts you to be part of its safe environment. Understanding your cat's preferences—like which petting spots they enjoy or how they prefer to be held—can make your interactions more rewarding for both of you.

Cats also bond through routines—because, after all, a schedule is crucial when you're running the household. Regular feeding times, play sessions, and quiet moments spent together are all opportunities to strengthen the emotional connection between you and your cat. These routines give cats a sense of stability and predictability, which is crucial for their emotional well-being. They are creatures of habit, and the more consistent you are with their routines, the more secure they feel.

Cats also bond with us through shared experiences. Ever notice your cat sitting beside you during a tough day or purring next to you when you're feeling down? It's because they're attuned to your emotions. Cats can sense when their humans need comfort, and they often offer their presence as a form of emotional support. This empathy is one of the reasons why many people find their bond with their cat so deep and meaningful.

Cats may also mirror their owners' behaviours—if you're feeling calm, they are more likely to relax, but if you're stressed, they may become anxious, too. It's like having an emotional barometer with whiskers.

Cats also bond by including their humans in grooming rituals. When a cat licks your hand or nuzzles against you, it's treating you like another cat in its family group. This grooming behaviour is a sign of deep trust and affection.

Additionally, cats often engage in playful behaviour as a way to bond. Engaging with your cat using their favourite toys can create a fun and emotionally enriching experience that strengthens your relationship. Just think of it as your cat's way of inviting you to their version of game night.

Tips for Strengthening Your Bond with Your Cat

- **Respect Their Boundaries**: Cats value their space. Always allow your cat to come to you on its own terms and avoid forcing interactions. Respecting their need for independence will make your cat more likely to approach you willingly. Pushing a cat to interact when it isn't in the mood can damage trust while giving it space can lead to more positive interactions. Creating an environment where your cat feels they have control over interactions is key to building trust—after all, cats thrive when they feel they are the ones making the decisions.

- **Engage in Interactive Play**: Playtime is important to a cat's emotional life. Using wand toys or laser pointers can help you bond while also providing mental and physical stimulation. Make sure to let your cat catch the toy sometimes to avoid frustration. Incorporating different types of play, like chasing, pouncing, or batting, can help cater to your cat's instincts and keep them engaged. Playtime should balance excitement and satisfaction—letting your cat have "victories" by catching the toy reinforces their natural hunting skills. Watching your cat go full ninja mode on a feather wand is always a joy.

- **Offer Positive Reinforcement**: Reward your cat with treats or affection when they display positive behaviour. This can help build trust and encourage them to seek out interactions with you. Positive reinforcement is a great way to turn routine interactions into meaningful bonding moments. For example, giving a treat after a grooming session can help your cat associate the experience with something positive. Consistent positive reinforcement also helps your cat feel safe and valued, making them more willing to interact—because who doesn't love a little reward now and then?

- **Provide a Safe Environment**: Ensure your cat can access various cosy hiding spots and elevated spaces. Cats feel safer when they have the ability to observe their environment from a secure location. Giving them options for retreats can reduce anxiety and make them feel more comfortable in your home. Creating a cat-friendly environment with climbing trees, window perches, and hiding nooks can help your cat feel more secure and happy. Elevated spaces also allow them to feel in control, which is important for their confidence—it's their version of having the high ground.

- **Learn Their Language**: Cats communicate through body language, vocalizations, and facial expressions. Learning what your cat is trying to tell you can help prevent misunderstandings and foster a deeper connection. Responding appropriately to their signals shows your cat that you understand them. For instance, if your cat gives you a slow blink, returning it can strengthen your bond by showing mutual trust. Understanding their cues will also help you avoid situations that could lead to stress or discomfort for your cat—basically, it's like learning a new language, but cuter.

Emotional Support from Cats: More Than Just Companionship

Cat Providing Emotional Support

Cats provide emotional support in subtle ways, often by simply tolerating our presence with quiet grace. They don't need grand gestures to tell us they're there for us. Their calm presence and gentle affection are soothing us, reducing our stress and anxiety without them needing to say a word. Dr. Linda Thompson, a veterinary psychologist, explains, "Cats have an incredible ability to sense when their owners need comfort, often providing silent companionship that can reduce anxiety and promote well-being."[4] It's like they have a sixth sense of knowing when we need a fluffy friend.

---

4. Dr. Linda Thompson, "The Therapeutic Role of Cats," Journal of Animal Companionship, 2022.

Dr Susan Brown's research found that "petting a cat not only lowers blood pressure but also releases endorphins, contributing to reduced stress levels in cat owners."[5] The rhythmic sound of a cat's purr can be incredibly calming and is thought to have healing properties, not just for the cat but for humans as well—like an adorable, fuzzy meditation session. This makes cats perfect companions for people who need an emotional boost or suffer from anxiety.

Cats also provide a sense of purpose and routine. The responsibility of feeding, grooming, and playing with a cat gives structure to the day, which can be particularly beneficial for people who feel isolated or struggle with depression. The bond between cats and humans is a mutually beneficial partnership built on trust, affection, and understanding.

In addition to their calming presence, cats also offer humour and entertainment, which can help lift their owners' spirits. Whether they're chasing an invisible bug, pouncing on a piece of lint, or curling up in amusing positions, cats naturally bring joy and laughter to their households. These lighthearted antics can brighten even the most challenging days, bringing a smile to your face when you need it most. Sharing these fun experiences strengthens your bond with your cat and adds positivity to your relationship.

Cat Curling Up on Lap

Cats also have an uncanny ability to know when their owners need extra comfort. Whether it's curling up on your lap during a tough day

---

5. Dr. Susan Brown, "Health Benefits of Cat Companionship," Veterinary Wellness Journal, 2021.

or nudging your hand for a gentle pet, these small gestures provide an emotional connection that can make a big difference in your well-being. This kind of empathy, combined with their playful nature, makes cats uniquely positioned to offer emotional support that goes far beyond simple companionship.

Conclusion: Embrace the Emotional Complexity of Cats

Cats are complex creatures with a rich emotional life that often goes unnoticed. You can strengthen your bond with your feline friend by learning to read their signals, respecting their boundaries, and engaging in meaningful interactions. Understanding their emotions allows you to appreciate the unique ways in which they express love and trust, making your relationship with them all the more fulfilling.

So, take the time to observe your cat, learn their language, and respond to their needs. The rewards of understanding and embracing your cat's emotional complexity are immense—a relationship built on trust, mutual respect, and affection that will bring both of you joy for years to come.

Cats are not just pets but companions with unique personalities and emotions. Their subtle displays of affection, gentle presence, and quiet loyalty make them truly special. By embracing their complexity, you open yourself to a world of companionship that is both rich and rewarding. Whether it's through shared routines, mindful petting, or simply sitting in silence together, your bond with your cat is something to be cherished. It's a bond built on trust, patience, and love, and it can transform your lives for the better.

Signs Your Cat

is Trying to Establish Dominance

Understanding what your cat is trying to communicate is key to building a strong relationship and maintaining a harmonious household. Picture this: your cat kneads your lap, and you think it's a loving gesture—when in reality, they're claiming you as their property, like a furry little landlord staking their territory. It's as if they're silently proclaiming, 'I own this lap, and don't you forget it.' These moments of miscommunication are what make cat ownership so hilariously unpredictable. Cats are masters of subtlety, using body language and behaviour to convey their feelings, needs, and intentions. In this chapter, we'll explore the signs your cat gives you and what they mean, focusing on three main behaviours: the stare-down, the tail twitch, and power plays.

Cat's Perspective

To truly understand the enigmatic behaviours of your feline companion, let's look at things from their perspective. Imagine your cat's internal monologue during these typical scenarios:

"When I stare at you long enough, I can almost see the wheels turning in your head—'Is it treat time, or am I being tested?' Spoiler: it's always treat time."

"Blocking the hallway isn't just about lounging comfortably; it's about control. I like to think of myself as a sentinel, deciding who gets the privilege of passing. And if I get a head scratch for my efforts, all the better."

"When I sit on your laptop, it's not because it's warm—although that's a nice bonus. It's my way of reminding you that I am, in fact, the most important thing in your life. Work can wait."

"You think I scratch the furniture because I'm bored? No, I scratch it to make it mine. Everything in this house is mine; I'm just letting you use it."

"When I bring you a 'gift' like that dead mouse, it's not just a present—it's a performance review. I'm showing you how it's done, so pay attention."

The Stare-Down: When Fluffy Means Business

The Stare-Down

Have you ever caught your cat staring at you with unblinking eyes, almost as if they are challenging you to a silent duel? Dr Emily Green, a feline behaviour specialist, explains that 'cats use staring as a means to assert dominance or gauge their human's response, essentially testing their boundaries.'[1] It's like a Western standoff, complete with the tumbleweed rolling by—except, of course, the stakes are whether or not you'll get up to refill their food bowl. This behaviour is known as the "stare-down," meaning several things. In the world of feline communication, a direct stare can be a display of dominance or curiosity. Your cat may be trying to establish its place in the social hierarchy, gauging your response to decide if you are worth its attention or if it needs to remind you who really runs the household. It's as if they're saying, 'Let's see if my human truly understands who's in charge here.'

To cats, staring is a powerful communication tool. When your cat stares at you, they might wait for you to act, perhaps to feed or engage them in play. On the other hand, a relaxed stare, accompanied by slow blinks, is a sign of trust. Dr Jane Smith states, 'Slow blinking is a cat's way of showing comfort and affection, akin to a human smile.'[2] Cats use slow blinking to convey comfort and affection, sometimes called a "cat kiss." To practice this, try slowly blinking at your cat and see if they return the gesture—it might feel a little silly, but it's a wonderful way to bond with your furry friend.

However, a hard, unyielding stare can indicate your cat is feeling threatened or defensive. To defuse this tension, you could offer a treat or distract them with a toy to shift their focus.

Some of the best distractions include feather wands, laser pointers, or even a crinkly ball—anything that can engage their hunting instincts and redirect their attention.

You might notice stare-downs between cats as they establish their pecking order in a multi-cat household. If the staring becomes too intense and is

---

1. Dr. Emily Green, *Understanding Cat Dominance*, Feline Behavior Journal, 2023.

2. Dr. Jane Smith, *Cat Comfort and Affection Signals*, Animal Behavior Insights, 2022.

accompanied by flattened ears or twitching tails, it's a good idea to step in and distract the cats to avoid escalation.

Staring contests between cats can be more than just about dominance; they are also a way to test each other's patience, courage, and willingness to back down. Understanding these subtle nuances can help facilitate a peaceful environment where each cat knows its role.

Staring is not always about conflict. An animal behaviourist, Dr Susan Brown, suggests, 'Recognizing these tail movements is crucial for maintaining a stress-free environment for your cat.[3] Sometimes, it can indicate deep interest or curiosity. When your cat gazes at you while you're doing something mundane, like reading or cooking, they may be genuinely curious about what you're up to. They are observing, learning, and connecting with you. This form of attentiveness is another way cats communicate their desire to be a part of your world. Responding to this type of staring with gentle interaction or even just talking to your cat can strengthen your bond and make them feel more integrated into your daily l ife.

The Tail Twitch: Decoding Feline Body Language

Watch the Different Tail
Reactions

The tail is one of the most expressive parts of a cat's body, and understanding its movements can give you great insight into your cat's mood. A common behaviour that puzzles cat owners is the tail twitch—much like a ticking time bomb, and you never know when it might go off. Dr Andrew Johnson notes that 'tail twitching can signify various emotions ranging from excitement to agitation, depending on the intensity and context.[4] It's like dealing with a moody coworker—you're never quite sure if they're about to snap or just deep in thought. Seeing your cat's tail twitching rapidly indicates they are agitated, excited, or slightly annoyed. This behaviour often occurs when your cat observes something intensely, such as a bird outside the window or a toy they are about to pounce on.

A gentle tail twitch, especially when your cat is resting, can indicate that they are relaxed but alert, ready to respond to whatever might happen next. However, a more pronounced, erratic tail movement might indicate irritation—perhaps they've had enough petting or are uncomfortable

---

4. Dr. Andrew Johnson, *Tail Language in Domestic Cats*, Journal of Feline Studies, 2021.

with the current situation. Understanding these subtle differences in tail behaviour can help you interact with your cat more effectively and avoid situations that might lead to stress or confrontation.

Cats also use their tails to communicate with other cats in the household. A high, gently waving tail often signals confidence and contentment, while a puffed-up tail is a clear sign of fear or aggression. When cats walk around with their tails held high, they exhibit pride and confidence, signalling to everyone around them—including other cats and humans—that they feel secure and in control. On the other hand, a cat with a low, tucked tail may feel submissive or anxious, and recognizing these signs can help you address their concerns.

In a multi-cat household, tail communication is crucial for maintaining harmony. Cats often use their tails to signal their intentions to other cats—whether it's an invitation to play or a warning to keep away. For example, when one cat approaches another with a slowly swishing tail, it's often a cautious invitation to engage. If the other cat responds with a quick flick, it usually means, 'Not now, I'm busy ruling this part of the house.' Understanding these signals can help you anticipate conflicts before they escalate, giving you an opportunity to intervene with distraction or redirection.

Tail language can also be directed at humans. If your cat's tail suddenly starts twitching while you're petting them, it's their way of saying, "I've had enough." Paying attention to these signals can prevent overstimulation and help maintain a positive relationship with your cat. On the other hand, if your cat approaches you with their tail held high, it's like they're waving a friendly hello—an invitation for some interaction and attention.

Expanding the Role of Humans

Cats may have us wrapped around their paws, but we humans need to understand our part in these power dynamics. Dr Linda Thompson emphasizes that 'humans often misinterpret feline behaviour, leading to power struggles that could be avoided by understanding a cat's natural instincts.[5] Here are some common mistakes that humans make when interpreting cat behaviour—and humorous corrections to help owners see things more clearly:

- **Mistake**: Thinking that a cat's affectionate nudge invites a cuddle.
  Correction: It's actually a royal decree to bring food. Proceed cautiously.

- **Mistake**: Assuming that a cat wants to share your blanket.
  Correction: The blanket belongs to the cat now—you're merely borrowing it.

- **Mistake**: Believing that the cat's meow means they're hungry.
  Correction: The meow is actually a demand for attention. They might not even be hungry—they just want to see you jump to action.

- **Mistake**: Thinking that when your cat lies on your laptop, they seek warmth.
  Correction: No, they're blocking you from doing anything that isn't about them. Your productivity is not their concern.

Owner Training: Who's Really in Charge?

Treat Levels

We often think we are training our cats, but it turns out they are training us. Below is a humorous evaluation scale to help you understand just how well you have been trained by your feline overlord:

- **Level 1**: You understand the concept of "treat time" but forget occasionally. Cat's judgment is stern.

- **Level 2**: You respond promptly to all meows, even if it means pausing a Zoom meeting. Respect points gained.

- **Level 3**: You rearrange your sleeping position to accommodate the cat. Congratulations, you are highly trained.

- **Level 4**: The cat has learned that you'll wake up at 5 a.m. without complaint. You're officially a graduate of Cat School.

- **Level 5**: You cancel plans because your cat needs extra cuddles. You've reached the pinnacle of feline approval.

- **Level 6**: You've trained yourself to open a can of food in complete silence at 3 a.m., just to avoid waking them up. You are now an elite servant.

Comparisons to Other Animals or Situations

Cats are unique in their approach to communication and asserting their dominance, especially when compared to other pets like dogs:

- **Dogs**: When a dog wants attention, they'll bring you a toy, wag their tail, and make puppy eyes that beg for playtime. Conversely, cats simply occupy your laptop and dare you to do anything about it. It's as if they're saying, "This is mine now. Good luck getting anything done, human."

- **Dogs**: A dog may look guilty after knocking something over. Cats? They will look you in the eye and knock over the same object again—just to see if you dare stop them. It's not mischief; it's performance art.

- **Dogs**: Dogs will follow commands because they want to please you. Cats? They'll only do what you want if it aligns with their own interests—otherwise, forget about it. If you ask a cat to do something, they'll give you a look that says, "You must be joking. What's in it for me?"

By embracing these unique feline behaviours, you'll come to appreciate your cat's individuality and the humour in their interactions with you.

The Power Play: How Cats Assert Their Authority

Welcome to the Wild World of Feline Power Plays

This subchapter explores how cats assert their authority within the household. From subtle body language cues to not-so-subtle demands for treats, our furry friends have a unique way of establishing their rank.

Natural-Born Leaders

First and foremost, it's important to understand that cats are natural-born leaders. They come from a long line of majestic hunters and rulers of the animal kingdom. When your cat struts around the house like they own the place, they're not just being arrogant but embracing their innate sense of authority. This sense of leadership is deeply ingrained in their instincts. Understanding this can help you appreciate their behaviours as more than just stubbornness.

Physical Displays of Power

One of the most common ways cats assert dominance is through physical displays of power. They may swat at another pet, arch their back, or puff up their fur to appear larger and more intimidating. Engaging in playful (but slightly aggressive) wrestling matches with other pets is also part of the game of cat supremacy. These behaviours communicate strength and establish boundaries with other animals, ensuring that their status within the household remains unchallenged.

Strategic Positioning

Cats also use strategic positioning to assert their authority. Have you ever noticed your cat sitting in doorways, hallways, or other frequently used areas? This is no coincidence—cats often position themselves in key locations to control the movement flow within the household. By placing themselves in these spots, they subtly remind everyone that they are in charge of their territory. They are, in effect, gatekeepers—like bouncers at an exclusive club—deciding who goes where and when. This behaviour is especially noticeable when a cat sits in a doorway, blocking another cat's or even a human's path, asserting dominance over that space.

The Softer Side of Authority

Don't be fooled by their tough exterior—cats have a softer side when asserting authority. These softer gestures are 'manipulative tactics' that keep us wrapped around their paws. They may cuddle up to you for extra attention or give you the sweetest purrs and headbutts to remind you who's in charge. By offering affection on their terms, cats demonstrate their fondness for you and subtly remind you of their role in the household hierarchy.

Resource Management

Another way cats assert their authority is by controlling resources—such as food, toys, and prime napping spots. Think of them as resource managers, ensuring they have the best allocation of household comforts. Have you ever noticed how your cat insists on eating first or always occupies the cosiest spot in the house? These actions are deliberate displays of control, reinforcing their position in the household hierarchy. This behaviour is especially prominent in multi-cat households, where competition for resources can be fierce. Ensuring that each cat has access to their own resources can help minimize conflict and reduce the need for overt displays of dominance.

Power Plays with Humans

Cats also engage in power plays with humans by demanding attention at specific times or in specific ways. For instance, your cat might jump onto your lap while you're working or insist on being petted when you're otherwise occupied. These behaviours are not just about seeking affection; they're a way for your cat to establish control over your time and attention—after all, who's really being trained here? By understanding and responding appropriately—sometimes indulging them, sometimes gently setting boundaries—you can maintain a healthy balance of power in your relationship.

Embrace the Power Play

Next time your cat demands to be fed at 5 a.m. or refuses to move from your spot on the couch, remember that it's all part of their grand scheme to maintain their rank in the household. Embrace the power play, and you'll be well on your way to establishing a harmonious relationship with your furry overlord—like a royal demanding tribute from their loyal subjects. Understanding and respecting your cat's need for authority can create an environment where both of you feel secure and respected. Your cat's power plays are not just about dominance—they establish a sense of order and stability that benefits everyone in the household. You can create a more peaceful and cooperative living arrangement by recognizing these behaviours and working with them rather than against them.

Conclusion

Feline power plays are a natural part of living with cats. By recognizing and respecting these behaviours, you can create a harmonious household where your cat feels secure in their role. Whether through a demanding meow, a gentle nudge, or a strategic nap spot, your cat always finds ways to assert authority. Embrace these behaviours, and use them to strengthen the bond you share with your cat. A balanced relationship built on mutual respect is the key to living happily with your furry overlord.

Every power play is also a chance to understand your cat better. Deeper companionship and trust come through understanding—which often means surrendering to their whims. By observing, learning, and responding to your cat's behaviours, you will gain insight into their unique personality and build a foundation of trust and affection that will make your lives richer and filled with countless amusing moments.

Strategies for Maintaining

Peace in a Multi-Cat Household

Living in a multi-cat household can be both rewarding and challenging. Imagine it like living with a group of quirky roommates—each with their own demands for the best lounging spots and the perfect mealtime service. Cats are territorial creatures, and understanding how to maintain harmony among them is key to creating a peaceful home. In this chapter, we will discuss several strategies to help ensure that each of your feline companions feels secure, respected, and content. We'll delve deeper into managing territory, establishing a natural hierarchy, and maintaining routines to promote a stress-free environment for all cats involved.

Playing Referee: When Cats Clash

Face off

Conflict between cats is natural, especially when trying to establish their place in the household hierarchy—it's like a feline version of a reality TV show, complete with dramatic standoffs and over-the-top gestures, where everyone wants to be the top cat.

- **Common Mistake**: Owners often mistake these clashes for serious fights rather than recognizing them as natural disputes.

- **Solution**: Try to identify if it's just a power struggle or something more serious before intervening. Picture one cat dramatically swatting the other away from the prime napping spot while the other cat stares back, plotting their next move—it's a never-ending saga of who gets to rule the couch.

When two cats clash, it's important not to panic. Instead, try to understand the reason behind the conflict. Is it a territorial dispute? Is one cat feeling threatened or anxious? Identifying the cause can help you determine how to intervene and prevent future clashes.

Sometimes, it may be enough to distract the cats with a toy or a treat—think of it as waving the white flag, except it's a feather wand. Feather wands, laser pointers, and other interactive toys can help redirect their energy into play, diffusing tensions. Remember, it's often about re-channelling the tension into something positive. Engaging your cats in a game they both enjoy can help them associate each other with fun rather than conflict.

However, if a particular cat consistently becomes the target of aggression, it's essential to provide that cat with safe spaces where they can retreat without fear of being pursued. Vertical spaces, like cat trees or shelves, can give your cats opportunities to escape and feel secure. Consider creating multiple vertical routes to ensure that even during tense moments, each cat has a way out that doesn't involve crossing paths with their rival.

Additionally, pay attention to body language cues that indicate escalating tension—such as flattened ears, puffed-up fur, or intense staring. Early intervention is key, and you can often prevent a full-blown altercation by stepping in with positive distractions before the situation gets out of hand. Be sure to monitor each cat's behaviour over time to understand patterns of conflict and identify ways to minimize them.

The Importance of Territory: Creating Zones of Control

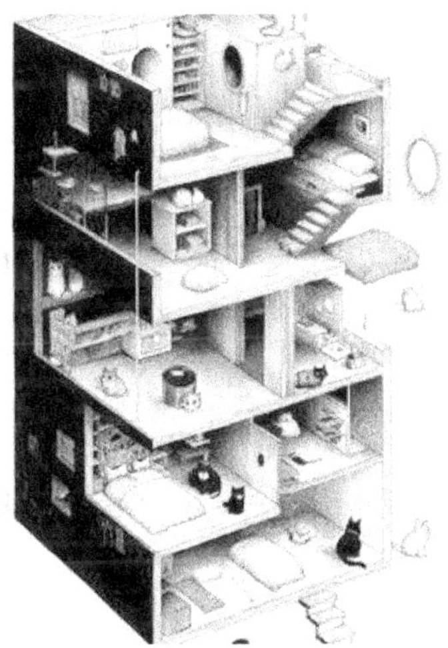

Different Zones: Creating the space

Cats are territorial animals, and in a multi-cat household, each cat needs to have its own space. Creating distinct zones for each cat can minimize territorial disputes and help maintain peace—after all, even cats need their own little 'studio apartments' to retreat to. Without their own space, you might find your cats battling it out for the best spot in the house, turning your living room into a feline version of musical chairs. These zones should include feeding stations, sleeping areas, and play areas that are exclusive to each cat. For example, you could designate specific rooms or corners of larger rooms for each cat, ensuring they have their own distinct territories. Understanding how to create these defined zones can help each cat feel secure and minimize competition.

- **Common Mistake**: Feeding cats too close to one another, which can create tension.

- **Solution**: Set up feeding stations in different parts of the home, ensuring that each cat has privacy during mealtime.

Feeding stations are particularly important.

Step-by-Step Implementation:

- Start by observing where each cat naturally gravitates during mealtime.

- Set up feeding stations in different home corners, ensuring each cat can comfortably eat without feeling threatened or disturbed.

- Gradually introduce the new feeding routine until all cats are comfortable.

Feeding cats in separate locations ensures that mealtimes don't become a source of conflict—think of it like hosting a chaotic dinner party where each guest needs their own private table to keep the peace. If one cat consistently eats from another's bowl, it can create tension and lead to more serious disputes. Feeding them in separate areas makes each cat feel secure while eating, minimizing competition. Elevated feeding areas can benefit cats that feel more comfortable eating in higher, less accessible locations. Feeding them in vertical or secluded areas can further reduce anxiety and help prevent food guarding.

Vertical spaces are also crucial for maintaining harmony. Cats feel more comfortable having vantage points to observe their environment from above. Installing cat shelves or providing cat trees allows them to control their space without direct confrontation. This vertical hierarchy helps establish order and reduces stress among cats. In addition to climbing spaces, consider placing resting areas in high locations where cats can enjoy uninterrupted nap time, free from the worries of other household cats intruding.

Another essential aspect of territory management is providing multiple litter boxes in different areas. A general rule of thumb is to have one litter box per cat plus an additional one. This prevents cats from feeling cornered while using a litter box and reduces the risk of litter box-related disputes. Each litter box should be placed in a quiet, low-traffic area to encourage usage and avoid confrontations.

Establishing a Hierarchy: The Dos and Don'ts

*Feline Hierarchy: With a Human
at the Base, Serving Everyone*

Establishing the Natural Hierarchy

Cats naturally establish their own social hierarchy, and it's essential not to disrupt this process. Think of it like a corporate ladder, except with more fur and fewer emails—one cat always wants to be the boss, and the others just have to deal with it. Trying to force a particular order among your cats is often counterproductive and can lead to more conflicts. Instead, observe how they interact and support the natural order that develops. Understanding their roles in the hierarchy allows you to work with their natural instincts rather than against them.

Respecting the Hierarchy

Respect the hierarchy by allowing the dominant cat to have first access to toys, food, or favoured resting spots—because nothing says 'top cat' like being the first to claim the comfiest bed. If this hierarchy isn't respected, you might find the dominant cat giving you the cold shoulder or dramatically sitting in front of the food bowl, clearly demanding that order be restored. This doesn't mean neglecting the other cats but rather ensuring that the established hierarchy is acknowledged to prevent friction.

Identifying the Dominant Cat

The dominant cat often exhibits certain behaviours, such as eating first, claiming the highest resting spots, or gently swatting other cats away from desirable locations. They may also initiate grooming sessions with other cats to assert dominance.

Providing Duplicate Resources

Providing duplicate resources—multiple scratching posts, litter boxes, feeding stations, and resting spots—can reduce competition and allow each cat to feel in control of its space. For example, if the dominant cat prefers a specific cat tree, make sure other equally appealing options are available for the others.

Avoiding Favoritism

Avoid favouring one cat over others. Cats are keenly aware of how their companions are treated, and favouritism can lead to jealousy and aggression—because, let's be honest, nobody throws a tantrum quite like a jealous cat, complete with dramatic sulking, strategic ignoring, and the occasional deliberate knocking of objects off shelves. Ensure each cat gets individual attention and equal opportunities for play and interaction.

Rotating playtime with each cat can help reinforce positive behaviours and create bonds without triggering competition. One effective approach is to schedule individual play sessions for each cat at different times of the day to help strengthen your bond with each one while minimizing the risk of conflict.

Watching for Signs of Bullying

It's also essential to watch for signs of bullying. When one cat consistently blocks access to resources or engages in behaviours that isolate another cat, it's important to intervene. Redirecting the bully with toys or interactive play can help, and ensuring the bullied cat has access to quiet areas where it can feel safe is crucial. Observing these interactions can help you adjust to the natural hierarchy without leaving any cat feeling vulnerable.

The Role of Routine: Consistency Is Key

Cats are creatures of habit, and a consistent routine can help reduce tension in a multi-cat household—think of it like working for a meticulous boss who likes everything 'just so.' Feeding, playtime, and grooming should occur at roughly the same times each day. Predictability makes cats feel more secure, reducing their need to compete for resources or attention. Establishing a steady routine is a simple but effective way to provide comfort and stability.

Changes to the household, such as new furniture or guests, can unsettle cats and lead to conflict. When changes are inevitable, introduce them gradually and provide extra comfort and reassurance to help your cats adjust. For example, if you need to add new furniture, place familiar items like their favourite blanket or toy near the new furniture to make it feel less intimidating. Let the cats explore it at their own pace, and reward them with treats for calm behaviour. Using pheromone diffusers during these changes can also help reduce anxiety and create a calming atmosphere.

A routine also includes daily interactive play sessions. According to Dr Emily Green, a feline behaviour specialist, establishing predictable play routines reduces stress and minimizes aggressive behaviour in cats.[1] According to Dr Jane Smith, an expert in animal behaviour, regular, scheduled playtime can simulate natural hunting behaviour and help cats release pent-up energy in a healthy manner.[2] Engaging in routine play with each cat provides an outlet for their energy and reinforces positive relationships among them. Scheduled playtimes give each cat something to look forward to and help them burn off excess energy, reducing the likelihood of redirected aggression toward each other.

Maintaining a grooming routine is another essential aspect of consistency. Dr. Andrew Johnson, a veterinarian, recommends that it reduce anxiety and reinforce bonds between cats.[3] Cats often groom each other to establish and reinforce bonds. However, in multi-cat households, not all cats may have this relationship. Regular grooming sessions with each cat can help stimulate that bond, reduce shedding, and create a calming experience that strengthens your relationship with each cat. Make sure to use a brush your cat enjoys, and be patient, especially with those less accustomed to being groomed.

Love and Attention: Balancing Affection Among All Cats

Cats need love and attention, but distributing that affection equally in a multi-cat household can be challenging. It's important to recognize each cat's unique personality and needs. Some cats are more independent, while others may require constant reassurance. Spending time with each cat individually helps build trust and shows them that they are valued household members.

- **Common Mistake**: Assuming all cats want the same kind of attention.

---

1. Dr. Emily Green, *The Benefits of Routine Play for Feline Well-Being*, Feline Behavioral Studies Journal, 2022.

2. Dr. Jane Smith, *Understanding Cat Behavior Through Play*, Animal Behavior Insights, 2021.

3. Dr. Andrew Johnson, *Grooming and Cat Anxiety: A Guide*, Veterinary Wellness Journal, 2023.

- **Solution**: Pay attention to each cat's preferences—some might love being held, while others prefer sitting nearby without direct contact.

Playtime is a powerful way to bond with your cats and provide an outlet for their energy. Use interactive toys to engage them, and rotate toys frequently to keep their interest. Grooming sessions are also an excellent opportunity to provide individual attention and reduce stress, as grooming can be a calming experience for most cats. For more timid cats, grooming sessions can be particularly valuable, as they provide a chance to build trust without overwhelming them with direct play.

Affection shouldn't always be about physical interaction. Some cats prefer just being near you without being touched. Recognize these preferences and respect them. Allowing a cat to share your space on their terms can be just as valuable as direct contact. Providing soft bedding near your workspace or favourite lounging area can help encourage a shy cat to be near you without the pressure of physical interaction.

Providing environmental enrichment can also be a form of affection. Cats love novelty, so switching up their environment by adding new toys, scratching posts, or even just rearranging existing items can make them feel valued and stimulate their curiosity. Aim to change or introduce new items every few weeks to keep things exciting and engaging for your cats. Catnip, puzzle feeders, or even a new cardboard box can be great additions to keep things fresh and exciting.

One-on-one cuddle time for the more affectionate cats can ensure they feel loved—especially when they demand it at the most inconvenient times, like when you're trying to have an important video call. For less affectionate cats, simply sitting quietly in the same room while they relax can demonstrate your care. Letting each cat know that they are special in their own way is the key to balancing affection and minimizing jealousy in a multi-cat home.

Conclusion: A Peaceful Home for All

Maintaining peace in a multi-cat household requires patience, understanding, and a willingness to adapt. Creating distinct zones for each cat, respecting their social hierarchy, and ensuring consistent routines can foster a harmonious environment where every cat feels secure. Each cat has unique needs and personalities, and by recognizing these differences, you can build a home where all your feline companions coexist happily.

Strategies for a Harmonious Multi-Cat Household
With these strategies in place, you can enjoy the rewards of a multi-cat household—where the dynamics are complex, but the love and companionship are immensely fulfilling. Keeping a watchful eye on their interactions, making necessary adjustments, and offering personalized attention to each cat will help maintain peace and harmony. Despite their differing personalities and preferences, your cats can learn to coexist peacefully when their needs are met and respected.

The Journey to Peaceful Coexistence
Remember, while it might take time for your cats to adjust and find their roles within the household, your efforts will pay off. Just be prepared for some dramatic moments along the way—cats love their flair for the theatrical! You'll be rewarded with the joy of watching them play, sleep, and even groom each other as they settle into their version of harmony. The journey to maintaining peace may have ups and downs, but the ultimate reward of a contented, multi-cat family is well worth it.

The Role of the Human

in the Feline Social Hierarchy

In a multi-cat household, the role of the human is absolutely crucial. You're the butler, referee, personal chef, and reluctant jester all rolled into one. Not only are you the caretaker, but also the mediator, peacekeeper, and provider. Your behaviour and decisions can significantly impact the well-being and dynamics of your feline family.

Adjusting feeding times to suit all cats' preferences, for example, can help reduce competition and create a more harmonious environment. This chapter will focus on cat owners' responsibilities in maintaining harmony, meeting each cat's needs, and ensuring a balanced environment that respects each cat's individuality. The more proactive and informed you are, the better you will be able to navigate the intricacies of a multi-cat home.

Cat Whisperer or Cat Servant: Finding Your Place

As a cat owner, your role fluctuates between being a 'cat whisperer' who understands and responds to subtle cues and a 'cat servant' who simply follows orders. This delicate balance can determine how well your cats adjust and coexist. Striking the right balance requires observation and a willingness to adapt to each cat's specific needs—like being a diplomat at an international conference, but with more fur and fewer language barriers.

For instance, understanding that one cat prefers solitary play while another enjoys group activities can lead to a happier household. Recognizing each cat's preferences ensures every cat feels understood and respected.

Learning to read your cats' signals is vital to being an effective caretaker. Dr Emily Green, a feline behaviour specialist, says, "Understanding subtle cues like tail flicks or narrowed eyes is key to fostering a positive relationship with your cat." [1]

It's like learning a secret language where a tail flick can mean anything from 'I'm mildly annoyed' to 'Bow before me, human!' From subtle body language to overt cues like vocalizations or swatting, understanding these signals allows you to respond appropriately. Misinterpreting or ignoring these cues can lead to unnecessary stress and tension.

For instance, if a cat is flicking its tail rapidly and you continue to pet them, they might become overstimulated and lash out, leading to a negative interaction for both of you. Nothing says 'chaos' like a confused cat family plotting a revolt—complete with dramatic tail flicks and judgmental stares. Each cat is an individual, and recognizing these nuances will help you address their needs more effectively.

One of the biggest challenges is realizing when your cat is trying to communicate something important versus when they are simply displaying typical cat behaviour. For instance, a cat that flicks its tail rapidly might be feeling irritated or overstimulated, while a slow blink can indicate a gesture of trust and affection. Observing these cues and

---

1. **Dr. Emily Green**, "Understanding Subtle Feline Cues," *Feline Behavioral Studies Journal*, 2022.

responding accordingly will foster a sense of mutual understanding and respect between you and your feline companions. Building this connection takes time, but the rewards are worth it—there's nothing quite like having a cat gaze at you with that slow, trusting blink that says, "You're alright, human."

It's essential to acknowledge that your cats view you as their all-powerful resource provider—think of yourself as a genie, but instead of a magic lamp, you have a can opener and endless treats. Dr. Jane Smith, a veterinary psychologist, explains, "Cats rely heavily on consistency from their humans to feel secure and valued."[2]

You provide food, entertainment, and comfort. Consistently fulfilling these roles helps your cats feel secure and valued. Sticking to feeding routines, play sessions, and grooming schedules reinforces your role as a trusted provider.

When your cats see you as reliable, they are less likely to feel insecure or compete for your attention. Inconsistent behaviours, like late feedings or ignoring playtime, can create anxiety and lead to negative behaviours like aggression or excessive vocalization.

Understanding your cats' preferences and personalities will help you decide how best to serve their needs. Some cats are more food-driven, while others crave physical affection or mental stimulation.

One cat might prioritize interactive playtime, while another may need a comfortable lap to rest on. Observing these distinctions allows you to adapt your approach to fulfil each cat's needs. Remember, each cat is different—some may enjoy a raucous play session with a feather wand, while others may prefer quiet moments by your side.

The Feline Social Ladder: Understanding Cat Hierarchies

Understanding the social ladder is key to maintaining harmony in a multi-cat household. Cats naturally form hierarchies with roles similar to an alpha, beta, and omega structure. You might have an 'Alpha' who

---

2. **Dr. Jane Smith**, "Consistency and Security in Cat Care," *Veterinary Psychology Review*, 2021.

always claims the highest perch, a 'Beta' who tries to keep the peace and an 'Omega' who tends to be submissive and often avoids conflicts. Each role has its own quirks and behaviours; recognizing them can help you manage household dynamics more effectively.

The Feline Social Ladder:
From Alpha to Omega

The Alpha cat expects the best spots in the house—usually the highest perch or the sunniest windowsill because nothing says 'top of the hierarchy' like basking in the warmth while everyone else looks on in envy. This cat might stare down others who dare to approach their territory, much like a boss guards their corner office.

On the other hand, the Beta will often groom other cats and try to defuse tensions. At the same time, the Omega is more likely to be submissive, often avoiding confrontations to maintain peace. Understanding these roles will help you cater to each cat's needs and intervene appropriately when the balance is threatened.

For example, if the Alpha starts picking on the Beta, a quick distraction with a toy can prevent a full-blown feline feud.

Multi-Cat Politics: Drama Unfolding in Your Living Room

The social dynamics in a multi-cat household can resemble a soap opera or a political drama. You may witness alliances forming, where two cats team up to keep a third away from a coveted nap spot. This is essentially 'Feline

Game of Thrones'—minus the dragons, but with plenty of dramatic glares and power plays. It's amusing to watch but can lead to tension if left unchecked.

Cats form these alliances for many reasons—sometimes it's to assert dominance, other times it's simply because they prefer the company of one cat over another. As a human, you can identify alliances by observing behaviours such as two cats consistently grooming each other or teaming up to block another cat from a resource.

Forming an Alliance

To prevent exclusion or bullying, ensure each cat has access to their own resources, like separate feeding stations and sleeping spots, and provide plenty of positive reinforcement when they interact peacefully. If you notice one cat consistently being left out, spend extra time playing with them or offer a special treat. As a human, it's your job to observe these dynamics and ensure no cat is being consistently left out or bullied. Providing duplicate resources, like multiple cosy spots or feeding areas, can help balance the power struggles and ensure everyone has a place to retreat.

Training the Human: From the Cat's Perspective

Human Training Milestones

While you're busy trying to train your cats, rest assured they are also trying to train you. From a cat's perspective, training their human is all about persistence—because who needs patience when you have relentless meows and the ability to look adorable while causing chaos? If they meow at 3 a.m. and you get up to feed them, they consider it a successful training session. Here are some "Human Training Milestones" from a cat's perspective:

- **Stage 1**: The human responds to my meows for food—eventually.

- **Stage 2**: The human knows my favourite napping spots and avoids disturbing me.

- **Stage 3**: The human wakes up at 3 a.m. to feed me without too much grumbling. Success!

- **Stage 4**: The human gives up their favourite chair because I have claimed it. Perfectly trained.

- **Stage 5**: The human knows the exact brand and flavour of treats I like and always keeps them stocked.

Adding a bit of humour and recognizing these behaviours can help you understand why your cat behaves as they do. It's all part of their plan to ensure they remain comfortable and in control. Remember, when your cat looks at you with those big eyes, they probably assess your performance as their personal assistant.

Humorous Comparisons to Other Pets

Cats vs Dogs

Cats are unique in their social dynamics, especially when compared to other pets like dogs—dogs want to please you, while cats want you to prove you're worthy of your time. Dogs might bring you a toy and look at you with hopeful eyes, begging for playtime. Conversely, cats will sit on your laptop, blocking your work, and stare at you as if daring you to do anything about it. It's not that cats don't want to play—they just want to do it on their own terms.

Dogs tend to fit seamlessly into a family structure, often happy to take orders and please their humans. Cats, however, have their own hierarchy and expect you to fit into it. They will decide when they want attention, where they want to sleep, and how they want you to serve them. Understanding these differences can help you appreciate the unique social structure that cats bring to a household. Unlike dogs, who are often eager to please, cats demand that you prove the worthiness of their affection.

They aren't impressed by simple tricks—they want devotion, patience, and a willingness to cater to their every whim.

Hierarchy Enforcement Tools: From the Human Perspective

The Wand of Distraction

Maintaining the hierarchy in a multi-cat household requires creative tools and strategies. Think of yourself as the keeper of peace, armed with 'The Wand of Distraction.' A feather wand can be your magic staff when tensions run high, effectively redirecting a cat's attention and diffusing confrontations before they escalate. The trick is understanding when to wield it—timing is everything.

Interactive play is one of the best ways to enforce hierarchy subtly. According to Dr Andrew Johnson, a specialist in animal behaviour, "Interactive play helps reduce tensions in multi-cat households by engaging all cats in a positive activity."[3] Using a laser pointer or a feather wand can work wonders in keeping all the cats engaged in a positive way. For example, if a dominant cat is bullying a more submissive cat, using the feather wand to engage both cats in play can help shift the focus and reduce tensions.

---

3. **Dr. Andrew Johnson**, "The Role of Interactive Play in Multi-Cat Households," *Animal Behavior Insights*, 2023.

Treats can also be a great way to manage hierarchy—rewarding positive interactions between cats helps reinforce good behaviour, like giving out bonuses to keep the peace in a very furry office. Just think of it as doling out "diplomatic treats" to keep the peace.

Conclusion: The Human Element in a Happy Multi-Cat Household

Your role as a human in a multi-cat household is multifaceted. You are a provider, peacekeeper, and source of comfort. Understanding when to step in or step back, creating a safe and enriching environment, and maintaining consistent routines can foster a harmonious atmosphere where all your cats feel secure and loved.

Remember, being a cat owner isn't just about providing food and shelter—it's about understanding the complex social dynamics at play and making decisions that benefit the group as a whole. With patience, attentiveness, and a bit of humour, you can ensure that your multi-cat household is a peaceful, joyful, and fulfilling home for you and your feline companions. Taking the time to understand the intricacies of each cat's personality, embracing your role as both servant and leader and using creative tools to maintain peace will ultimately lead to a happier home for everyone involved. Your cats might think they rule the house—and, let's face it, they probably do—but they can rule in harmony with your gui dance.

The Cat's Meow

Communicating Within the Hierarchy

Have you ever wondered what your cat tries to tell you when they meow, purr, or hiss? Cats use vocalizations as their primary way to communicate with their human companions, and each sound they make carries a different meaning. Experts like Dr John Bradshaw explain that cats use different sounds to express various needs and emotions, making it crucial for owners to learn to interpret these vocalizations. [1] For example:

- **Alpha Cats**: May use loud, assertive meows to establish dominance.

- **Beta Cats**: Use moderate meows to communicate needs without appearing aggressive.

- **Omega Cats**: Often use softer meows to indicate submission or seek reassurance.

---

1. Dr. John Bradshaw, "Cat Sense," Feline Behavioral Studies Journal, 2013.

A short, sharp meow might indicate excitement, while a low, drawn-out meow could signal discomfort. In this chapter, we'll dive into the quirky and fascinating world of feline vocalizations, breaking down what your cat's various sounds mean and how you can better understand what they are trying to say. From meows and purrs to the occasional hiss, get ready to decode the mysteries behind your furry friend's communication skills and become fluent in "cat."

Vocalizations: What Your Cat's Sounds Really Mean

Have you ever wondered what your cat tries to tell you when they meow, purr, or hiss? Different types of cats—alpha, beta, or omega—may use these vocalizations in various ways to express their position in the household. In this subchapter, we will dive into the world of feline vocalizations and uncover the hidden meanings behind your cat's sounds. Get ready to decode the mysteries of your furry friend's communication skills, including their meows, purrs, and hisses!

Meowing

- **Attention Meows**: Sometimes, a cat's meow can indicate something more serious, like alerting you to an empty water bowl, a potential health issue (such as dental pain or an upset stomach), or a problem in their environment that needs your attention. The way this meow sounds can vary depending on whether the cat is an alpha, beta, or omega.

  - **Alpha Cats**: Often use a loud and commanding tone to demand immediate attention.

  - **Beta Cats**: Will typically meow in a moderate tone, conveying their needs without appearing too pushy.

  - **Omega Cats**: Use softer and more hesitant meows, often indicating insecurity or a need for reassurance.

- **Communication with Humans**: Meowing is their way of communicating with humans, not other cats. So, the next time your cat meows incessantly, they might be trying to tell you they need attention or affection. Or maybe they're just practising their opera skills—who knows?

- **Different Types of Meows**: Meowing can vary in pitch and intensity, with different types of meows indicating different needs. A loud, demanding meow might mean, "Feed me now." A softer, more insistent meow could be a request for affection or playtime.

Understanding Meows: Different types of meows can reveal the hierarchy and needs of cats. Experts like Dr Emily Watson explain that alpha cats often use loud, demanding meows to assert dominance, while beta and omega cats communicate their needs with more moderate or submissive tones. [2] Alpha cats often use loud, demanding meows to assert dominance, while beta and omega cats communicate their needs with more moderate or submissive tones.

- **Alpha Cats** Often use loud and demanding meows to assert their dominance and claim resources. These meows can be insistent and may be accompanied by body language that reinforces their place at the top of the hierarchy. Alpha cats may use prolonged, repetitive meows to demand attention, making their needs known until they are satisfied.

- **Beta Cats** May meow to communicate their needs without challenging the hierarchy.

- **Omega Cats** Use softer, more submissive meows, often seeking comfort or reassurance.

Distinguishing between these different vocalizations can help you understand what your cat wants and respond appropriately. Just remember, the more you understand, the less likely you will end up with a paw in your face at 3 a.m.

Purring

- **Contentment Purring**: The soothing sound of a cat purring is often a sign of contentment and relaxation. Experts like Dr Jane Miller note that purring can indicate a cat's satisfaction and comfort, which is especially common in relaxed environments. [3] Alpha cats may purr loudly to assert their satisfaction and control over their environment, while omega cats may use a quieter purr to communicate comfort or seek approval. Your cat is basically saying, "I'm happy and comfortable right now, so keep the chin scratches coming."

- **Self-Soothing Purring**: Purring isn't always a sign of happiness. Cats may also purr to self-soothe during stressful situations. Experts like Smith et al. highlight how the purring vibration can help them cope with pain or discomfort. [4]

- **Beta Cats**: May purr to maintain a balanced environment without challenging the hierarchy.

- **Omega Cats**: Often purr as a stress relief mechanism when feeling intimidated by more dominant cats. They may also purr when in pain or feeling unwell, using the vibration to comfort themselves. For example, a cat might start purring after a minor injury, using the vibration to self-soothe and help reduce their discomfort. The act of purring can lead to the release of endorphins, which help reduce pain and promote a sense of well-being, making it an effective self-soothing mechanism.

- **Context Matters**: Understanding the context of the purring—whether your cat is in your lap enjoying a petting session or hiding in a corner—can provide valuable clues about their emotional and physical state. It's all about reading the room,

---

3. Dr. Jane Miller, "Understanding Feline Emotions," Cat Behavior Research Review, 2021.

4. Smith et al., "Purring as a Self-Soothing Mechanism," Journal of Feline Health, 2020.

or in this case, reading the purr. And sometimes, reading the purr also means knowing when it's time for a break—after all, even the best cat servants need a moment of rest!

Hissing

- **Threatened or Scared**: When your cat hisses, it's a clear sign that it is feeling threatened or scared. The intensity of the hiss may also vary depending on the cat's personality:

    - **Alpha Cats**: Will hiss loudly and pair it with assertive body language to deter threats.

    - **Beta Cats**: Use a moderate hiss to express discomfort, often in an attempt to maintain peace.

    - **Omega Cats**: Have a more defensive hiss, often paired with submissive body language, to signal fear rather than aggression. It's their way of saying, "Back off. I'm not in the mood for cuddles right now."

- **Giving Space**: If your cat starts hissing, give it some space and approach it later when it feels more at ease. You can also invest in some catnip—that usually does the trick!

- **Defensive Behaviour**: Cats also hiss to ward off potential threats. Hissing is often accompanied by other signs of fear or aggression, such as flattened ears, a puffed-up tail, or an arched back.

- **Respect the Hiss**: By understanding these signals, you can learn when to give your cat the space they need and avoid pushing them into uncomfortable situations. For example, if your cat starts hissing when another pet approaches, giving them space has helped avoid many potential conflicts. Redirecting their attention with a toy or simply stepping back can prevent escalating tensions and keep the peace. Respect the hiss—it's their version of "Do Not Disturb."

Understanding your cat's vocalizations is key to navigating their social dynamics and building a stronger bond with your feline friend.

Remember, alpha, beta, and omega cats will vocalize differently depending on their personalities and position within the household.

You can better understand their needs and strengthen your relationship by noticing their meows, purrs, and hisses.

So, next time your cat starts meowing non-stop, remember they might be telling you they love you—or just demanding food. Embrace the quirky world of feline communication and enjoy endless conversations with your furry companion.

The more you learn to interpret their vocal cues, the more effectively you'll respond to their needs, leading to a happier and more harmonious home. And who knows—you might even become fluent in "cat." But don't expect it to get you out of trouble when they catch you petting the neighbour's dog.

Purring is one of the most soothing sounds for cat owners, but what does it really mean?

Often, purring is a sign of contentment and relaxation—your cat's way of saying, "I'm happy and comfortable right now, so keep the chin scratches coming."

However, purring isn't always about happiness. Cats may also purr when they're in pain or feeling unwell, using the vibration to comfort themselves. This act of purring releases endorphins, which help reduce pain and promote well-being, making it an effective self-soothing mechanism.

And let's not forget the strategic side of purring—sometimes, it's simply a clever ploy to get more treats or extra attention.

To truly understand your cat, it's important to consider the context—whether they're in your lap enjoying petting or hiding in a corner. It's all about reading the situation, or in this case, reading the purr. Hissing is your cat's way of saying, "Back off, I'm not in the mood for cuddles right now." Experts like Dr Sarah Thompson explain that hissing is a clear indication of discomfort or perceived threat, often accompanied by physical signals like an arched back or flattened ears. [5]

This is often accompanied by physical signs such as an arched back, flattened ears, or a puffed-up tail, which help emphasize their discomfort. It's a clear sign that they're feeling threatened or scared.

Hissing is also a defensive behaviour used to ward off potential threats, often accompanied by flattened ears, a puffed-up tail, or an arched back. If your cat starts hissing, it's best to:

- **Give Them Space**: Approach later when they feel more at ease.

- **Offer Catnip**: This may help calm them down.

By understanding these signals, you can learn when to give your cat the necessary space and avoid pushing them into uncomfortable situations. Respecting these signals can lead to a more trusting relationship, making your cat feel safer and more comfortable around you, which ultimately strengthens your bond. Respect the hiss—it's their version of "Do Not Disturb," and ignoring it might just earn you a spot on their list of grudges. In conclusion, understanding your cat's vocalizations can help you navigate their social hierarchy within the household.

You can better communicate with your feline friend and strengthen your bond by paying attention to their meows, purrs, and hisses.

So, next time your cat starts meowing non-stop, remember they're just trying to tell you they love you (or they want food—it could go either way).

Embrace the quirky world of feline communication and enjoy endless conversations with your furry companion.

The more you learn to interpret their vocal cues, the more you'll be able to respond to their needs effectively, leading to a happier and more harmonious relationship.

---

5. Dr. Sarah Thompson, "Feline Defensive Behaviors," Feline Behavioral Studies Journal, 2020.

And who knows—you might even become fluent in "cat." Don't expect
it to get you out of trouble when they catch you petting the neighbour's
dog.

The Dual Nature of Purring

The Power of Purring: Comforting or Commanding?

In the world of cats, a mysterious power has fascinated and mystified cat
owners for centuries—the power of purring.

Is purring a comforting gesture from our feline friends or a subtle
command to establish their dominance within the household? Let's dive
into this purr-fectly intriguing topic. First and foremost, let's address the
comforting aspect of purring.

Cat owners are all too familiar with the soothing sound of their cat's purr
as they curl up in their laps or snuggle close during nap time. It's like
a gentle massage for the soul, a warm fuzzy blanket of reassurance that
everything is right in the world. So, can our furry friends simply express
their love and contentment through their purring?

Or are they secretly plotting their next move to assert their dominance? On
the other hand, some cat behaviour experts, such as Dr John Bradshaw,
speculate that purring may actually be a form of subtle manipulation and
control. [6] Picture this: your cat purrs loudly as you prepare their dinner,
giving off the impression of contentment and gratitude.

---

6. Dr. John Bradshaw, "Cat Sense," Feline Behavioral Studies Journal,
   2013.

But in reality, they may be using their purr as a way to command you to serve their meal faster, asserting their dominance as the ruler of the household. Sneaky, right?

Cats are known to use purring strategically to signal contentment and elicit a specific response from their human companions. For example:

- **Solicitation Purring**: A cat might use 'solicitation purring' when they want food or extra attention, knowing that this particular purr will get the desired response from their human. This "solicitation purring" often has a higher frequency, which some researchers believe is specifically designed to grab a human's attention and prompt them to take action.

Whether purring is a comforting gesture or a commanding tactic, one thing is certain—it's a powerful tool in your cat's arsenal. Understanding the nuances of your cat's purring can help you navigate their household social hierarchy and establish your rank as the ultimate cat whisperer.

Cats are complex creatures whose purring can convey multiple messages depending on the situation:

- **Alpha Cats**: May purr to display satisfaction and dominance.

- **Beta Cats**: Often purr to maintain a balanced environment, neither asserting dominance like alpha cats nor seeking reassurance like omega cats.

- **Omega Cats**: Might purr as a self-soothing behaviour in a stressful environment.

For instance, a cat that purrs while being petted is likely expressing comfort, but if they purr while hiding or after a fall, they may be trying to self-soothe. The more in tune you are with your cat's body language and the context of their purring, the better you'll respond appropriately.

Remember, a well-timed ear scratch might be all it takes to stay in your cat's good graces. Purring also has physical benefits for cats.

Studies have suggested that the vibrations produced by purring may have physical benefits for cats:

- **Healing**: The vibrations may promote healing and reduce pain.

- **Stress Relief**: This could explain why cats often purr when they are injured or unwell. This natural healing mechanism might be one of the reasons why cats are known for their resilience and ability to recover from injuries. By understanding the different contexts in which cats purr, you can gain deeper insights into their health and well-being, allowing you to provide better care for your feline friend.

And, of course, it doesn't hurt that they've got you wrapped around their paw in the process.

In conclusion, the power of purring is a fascinating phenomenon showcasing our beloved cats' complex social dynamics. Whether they're using it to comfort or command us, one thing is certain—we are at the mercy of their adorable purring prowess. So, embrace the purr and revel in the joy of being owned by your furry feline overlord.

Remember, in the world of cats, purring is not just a sound—it's a language of love, manipulation, and dominance all rolled into one. By paying close attention to your cat's purring and the context in which it occurs, you can unlock the secrets of their communication and build a stronger, more trusting bond.

And who knows? One day, you might figure out if they are plotting to take over the world—or just the comfy spot on the couch.

Cat Body Language at a Glance

Body Language: Reading Between the Whiskers

Welcome, cat owners, to the fascinating world of body language!

As we all know, cats are masters of communication without saying a word. From the flick of a tail to the twitch of a whisker, our feline friends have a whole language of their own.

Today, we will focus on one of the most telling indicators of your cat's mood and status within the household—their whiskers. If you've ever wondered what your cat thinks, just look at those whiskers.

Like furry antennas, they pick up on all the subtle cues and signals in your cat's environment. Are they relaxed and outstretched? Congratulations, your cat is feeling comfortable and confident.

You might also notice other relaxed body language cues, such as a slow blink or a gently swaying tail, indicating that your cat is at ease.

But if those whiskers are pulled back close to their face, watch out—your cat may feel anxious or threatened. Omega cats often exhibit this behaviour when they sense a challenge from an alpha cat. It's like a mood ring but on their face! But it's not just about their feelings—a cat's whiskers can also tell you much about their place in the social hierarchy at home.

Like a peacock flaunting its feathers, a cat with outstretched whiskers may show curiosity, interest, or even a hint of dominance. They say, "I'm the boss around here, so watch out."

On the other hand, a cat with their whiskers pulled back may feel more submissive, deferring to the alpha cat in the household. It's like a game of Whisker Wars, with each cat vying for the top spot. Whiskers aren't the only part of your cat's body language worth observing. A cat's tail, ears, and even their eyes can provide valuable insights into their mood and intentions. Different types of cats also use body language uniquely: alpha cats may display upright, confident postures, while omega cats might show submissive signals like a lowered tail or crouching.

A cat's tail, ears, and even their eyes can provide valuable insights into their mood and intentions. For instance, a cat with an upright tail that has a slight curve at the tip usually feels friendly and approachable, while a tail that is puffed up indicates fear or aggression.

Similarly, ears that are facing forward signal interest, whereas flattened ears indicate fear or irritation. By combining these cues with the whisker position, you can better understand your cat's emotional state.

For example, a friend noticed her cat's ears were flattened, and whiskers were pulled back while another cat approached. By recognizing these cues together, she could intervene and prevent a fight before it started. Understanding your cat's body language can also help you prevent conflicts between your cats or with other pets.

For example, if you notice one cat's whiskers are pulled back while another cat is approaching, it might be a sign of an impending conflict. In such cases, redirecting their attention with a toy or treat can help prevent a skirmish.

Paying attention to these subtle cues can go a long way in maintaining peace and harmony in a multi-cat household. This can include preventing fights or recognizing when a cat needs alone time. Recognizing whether an alpha, beta, or omega cat displays these cues is crucial to managing their interactions effectively.

So, next time you're trying to decipher your cat's behaviour, don't forget to pay attention to those whiskers. They may be small, but they pack a big punch when it comes to understanding your cat's social dynamics.

And who knows, maybe you'll even pick up a few tricks on building a deeper connection with your cat—just make sure to leave the whisker twitching to the experts. After all, in the world of cats, it's all about reading between the whiskers.

By observing and interpreting these small but significant signals, you'll gain a deeper appreciation for your cat's unique personality and strengthen the bond you share with them, creating a more harmonious home for everyone. And remember, failing to understand these signals might lead to unexpected furniture takeovers or royal sulks—best to stay on their good side!

Feline Friendship and Bonding

Just getting on together

Cats are known for their independence, but they can also form strong bonds with humans and other animals—even the aloof alpha cats, the cautious beta cats, and the gentle omega cats.

While their independence is undeniable, the friendships they form can be surprisingly deep and rewarding.

For instance, you might have seen two cats rubbing their faces together or gently touching their noses—small gestures that speak volumes about their affection.

These seemingly simple actions are expressions of trust and love, marking the beginning of a strong bond. While they may not display affection in the same obvious way that dogs do, cats have their own unique ways of showing love and forming friendships. It's these understated yet meaningful gestures that make feline friendships so special.

In this chapter, we'll explore the signs of true feline friendship, how to encourage positive interactions, and how to foster a loving and peaceful multi-cat household.

Whether you are dealing with an assertive alpha, a balanced beta, or a sensitive omega cat, each feline has their own way of relating to others.

Get ready to discover the softer side of your feline companions and learn how to help them develop meaningful relationships. You'll learn about creating a positive environment where each cat feels secure and confident enough to share affection.

And remember, even the most aloof feline can surprise you with unexpected affection—sometimes more than you'd imagine as if they suddenly decided to bestow their 'royal grace' upon you. In those moments, the feline personality's uniqueness shines brightest.

Cats are, after all, creatures full of contradictions. One moment, they're perched on the highest shelf, giving you that look of superiority; the next, they're curled up in your lap, purring softly and reminding you why you adore them. The alpha cat may maintain their air of authority, the beta cat plays the role of peacekeeper, and the omega cat prefers staying out of the spotlight, yet all of them can melt your heart in their own way.

They're less like benevolent rulers and more like self-proclaimed emperors who know when to charm their way back into your good books. Understanding their friendships, both with each other and with you, can reveal a lot about the nature of these enigmatic creatures. Experts like Dr. Emily Green explain that recognizing how cats express friendship is key to fostering a multi-cat household. [1] By recognizing and responding to these cues, you create an environment that fosters trust and companionship.

Whether the alpha cat asserts its leadership, the beta cat tries to mediate and keep the peace, or the omega cat just wants to nap undisturbed, there's always a story unfolding—often as dramatic as any royal court intrigue. Each cat has its own role in the household, and understanding these roles helps foster a peaceful coexistence.

---

1. Dr. Emily Green, "Understanding Subtle Feline Cues," Feline Behavioral Studies Journal, 2022.

Have you ever wondered what's going on behind those inscrutable eyes? Cats have their own secret ways of bonding; part of the fun is figuring it out. Every blink, purr, or head bump allows you to connect with your feline friends on a deeper level.

In this chapter, you will learn the signs of a true feline friendship and how to encourage positive interactions in your multi-cat home actively. So buckle up, prepare your treat stash, and dive into feline friendship's delightful complexities. Understanding these dynamics will create harmony and reveal the deeply rewarding experience of seeing your cats build unique relationships.

Signs of True Feline Friendship

Signs of True Feline Friendship

Feline friendships can be subtle but incredibly rewarding. For example, a gentle head bump or a slow blink from one cat to another is a small yet significant sign that they are building trust and affection. Dr Sarah Thompson describes these behaviours as crucial bonding signals. Unlike dogs, who often wear emotions on their paws, cats show affection in more understated ways. [2] Here are some of the key signs that your alpha, beta, and omega cats are becoming the best of buddies:

- **Mutual Grooming**: When cats groom each other, it shows trust and affection. Grooming is a bonding behaviour that strengthens social connections. If you notice your cats grooming each other, it

---

2. Dr. Sarah Thompson, "Feline Trust and Affection," Journal of Feline Behavior, 2021.

means they have accepted one another as part of their social group.

Grooming sessions are a way for one cat to say, "You're part of my crew now," reinforcing a bond that goes beyond mere cohabitation. The alpha cat may initiate the grooming, showing care for their fellow feline, while the beta cat is happy to reciprocate. The omega cat might hesitantly join in, feeling reassured.

- **Sleeping Together**: Cats are most vulnerable when they are asleep. If they choose to sleep close to each other—or even better, curled up together—this shows a high level of trust.

Does your cat have a favourite napping buddy yet? It means they feel safe in each other's presence. They aren't just sharing warmth; they're sharing a bond. Watching two cats snoozing in a heap of intertwined paws and tails is like witnessing a feline declaration of love. It says, "I trust you enough to let my guard down completely." The omega cat often feels safest nestled between the alpha and beta, while the alpha may sleep on the perimeter to keep a watchful eye.

- **Playing Together**: Play is a great indicator of friendship. When cats engage in playful behaviour without aggression, they are comfortable and enjoy each other's company.

Dr John Bradshaw notes that play is essential for social bonding among cats, especially in multi-cat environments. The alpha cat may lead the charge, initiating the game, while the beta cat follows along, and the omega cat joins in (sometimes reluctantly), hoping not to get caught in the crossfire.[3]

- **Tail Touching**: Cats that are comfortable with each other may touch or intertwine their tails. It's like a feline version of holding hands—a simple but significant gesture of closeness.

Tail touching is their way of saying, "I've got your back." Sometimes, you might catch them sitting side by side with their tails wrapped around each other, almost as if they're keeping each other warm or simply showing their unity. The alpha may extend their tail first, with

---

3. Dr. John Bradshaw, "The Dynamics of Feline Play," Feline Interaction Review, 2020.

the beta cat confidently reciprocating and the omega cat joining in
when they feel comfortable.

If your cats are displaying these behaviours, congratulations! You've got
yourself a true feline friendship. Don't expect them to start a friendship
bracelet club anytime soon, although a shared favourite toy might be close
enough. Remember, cats are all about subtlety, and sometimes, those quiet
moments of companionship are more profound than any grand gesture.
And while the alpha, beta, and omega dynamics are always in play, their
bonds are undeniable.

Feline Playtime Bonding

Cat Companionship: Encouraging Positive Interactions

Creating a positive environment where alpha, beta, and omega cats
feel comfortable with each other can be challenging, especially when
introducing a new cat to an established household. Experts like Dr.
Jane Miller emphasize the importance of gradual and well-managed
introductions. [4]

Here are some tips to encourage positive interactions and companionship
between your alpha, beta, and omega feline friends:

- **Slow Introductions**: When introducing a new cat, take it slow.
  Use scent swapping (like exchanging bedding) to help them get
  used to each other's smell before meeting face to face. Cats need
  time to adjust; a gradual introduction will help prevent initial

---

4. Dr. Jane Miller, "Multi-Cat Introductions: A Step-by-Step Guide,"
   Cat Behavior Research, 2019.

hostility.

Think of it as giving them space to feel comfortable before they share territory—like giving visiting royalty time to adjust before the grand meeting. The alpha may assert control early, while the beta helps ease the transition, and the omega cat simply needs extra patience.

- **Separate Spaces**: Provide each cat with its own space—a cosy nook, a perch, or a quiet hiding spot. Cats value their personal space, and having areas they can call their own helps prevent territorial disputes and fosters a sense of security.

After all, everyone needs a retreat, and for cats, it might be a sunny windowsill or the top of a bookshelf. Think of these spaces as individual safe zones—places they can recharge when socializing becomes overwhelming.

- **Shared Positive Experiences**: Encourage shared activities that all three cats can enjoy, such as interactive play with wand toys or puzzle feeders that they can explore together.

The alpha cat might hog the first few rounds, but with enough patience, even the omega cat will get a chance to join in. The goal is to create positive associations with being near each other.

- **Rewarding Good Behavior**: Use treats and praise when your cats interact peacefully. Rewarding them during moments of calm coexistence reinforces positive behaviour and helps build a friendly relationship over time.

According to Dr. Emily Watson, consistent rewards can effectively shape peaceful coexistence.[5]

- **Respect Individual Preferences**: Just like humans, cats have different personalities. Some may be more social, like the confident alpha cat, while others are shy or reserved, like our sweet omega.

---

5. Dr. Emily Watson, "Positive Reinforcement in Multi-Cat Households," Feline Behavioral Insights, 2020.

Respecting each cat's individual temperament and not forcing interactions can make all the difference in fostering companionship. Do you notice when your cat prefers solitude? Recognizing these moments is key to letting friendships develop naturally.

The Importance of Space

The Challenges of Feline Friendship

Not all cats are social butterflies—some are more like social tortoises, taking their time to warm up to others. Here are some common challenges when it comes to feline friendships and how to overcome them:

- **Territorial Behavior**: Cats are territorial by nature, and introducing a new cat can trigger defensive behaviour. To manage this, ensure plenty of resources (food bowls, litter boxes, resting spots) spread throughout the home. This reduces competition and helps each cat feel secure in its territory. More resources mean fewer reasons to argue—nobody likes to share their favourite napping spot. The more you cater to their needs, the more they will be at ease, reducing overall tension.

- **Bullying**: Sometimes, one cat may dominate or bully another, especially during the early stages of introduction. Keep an eye on their interactions, and if you notice persistent aggression, intervene by redirecting the dominant cat's attention with a toy. Providing extra attention to the more submissive cat can also help balance the power dynamic. Remember, in the feline world, sometimes it's about who gets the prime perch, and you might need to play the role of diplomat. Consider using barriers or time-outs if needed—sometimes, giving the dominant cat a break can help diffuse tensions.

- **Personality Clashes**: Cats, like people, have distinct personalities. Sometimes, two cats just don't click. In these cases, it's important to give them time and space. Forced interactions can do more harm than good, so let them find their own way of coexisting, even if it means they never become best friends. Coexistence without chaos is still a win! Celebrate the moments they tolerate each other rather than focus solely on becoming best buddies—sometimes, a peaceful truce is just as good as friendship.

Managing Feline Challenges

Remember, cats are complex creatures, and building friendships takes time. Patience is key—and so is a stash of treats for when they finally start getting along! Keep celebrating those small milestones—every peaceful nap and every shared sunbeam is a step toward a happier feline family. Your cats may not become best friends overnight, but those moments of quiet companionship add up, gradually creating a harmonious home.

Conclusion: Feline Friendship for a Happier Home

Building strong bonds between your cats isn't always easy, but the rewards are well worth the effort. When your feline companions trust and enjoy each other, it leads to a more peaceful and harmonious household. Understanding the signs of feline friendship and encouraging positive interactions can help your alpha, beta, and omega cats develop lasting relationships—even if those relationships sometimes involve the occasional hiss or paw swipe. After all, even in the feline world, friends have their moments!

Think of it as their version of "hiss and makeup"—a brief spat followed by a calm truce, often ending with a shared nap or mutual grooming session.

Celebrate the small victories:

- A shared nap spot between your cats.

- It's a game of chase that doesn't end in chaos.

- Your omega cat joining in play without feeling threatened.

- Your alpha cat allows the beta to lead a game.

Each of these milestones contributes to a more harmonious household. With time, patience, and plenty of treats, your cats may just become the best of friends—or at least learn to tolerate each other with minimal drama. And hey, even a little tolerance goes a long way regarding feline harmony.

Here's to more purrs, fewer hisses, and a household full of happy cats. Keep those treats handy, maintain a sense of humour, and never forget that every small step counts. After all, in the world of cats, true friendship is a journey filled with curiosity, respect, and just the right amount of distance to make it work.

Cats and Dogs

Navigating Cross-Species Social Dynamics

Canine Intruders: A Feline's Perspective

Have you ever noticed how a cat's expression shifts when a dog enters the room? It's as if they're wondering, "Who let the barking machine in here?" From the cat's point of view, a dog's arrival is like inviting chaos into a carefully curated kingdom. Cats, who pride themselves on their elegance and composure, see dogs as loud, clumsy, and too eager to please—traits that can be baffling and irritating to their refined sensibilities. Imagine living in a serene art gallery, only to have a bouncy, slobbering tourist burst in, eager to touch everything. That's the essence of a cat's experience when a dog enters their domain.

And yet, sometimes, just sometimes, an unlikely alliance forms. It's a bit like that one neighbour who always pops by uninvited—annoying at first, but eventually, you might miss them when they're gone. For cats, the secret to surviving a canine intruder lies in mastering the art of control—control over their environment, themselves, and ultimately, the dog.

According to Dr. John Bradshaw, a feline behaviour specialist, "Cats rely on high vantage points to feel safe around dogs. Providing vertical space, like cat trees or shelves, helps ease initial anxiety." [1]

First Impressions: The Art of Ignoring

Different Cats Reacting to a
Dog's Arrival

For cats, the key to getting along with dogs is to pretend they don't exist. Cats take different approaches depending on their role within the hierarchy:

- **Alpha Cats**: Take up a high perch—somewhere they can look down upon the newcomer and judge silently. It's not an outright rejection; it's a strategic assessment, much like a feline diplomat deciding if this new creature deserves a visa to Catland.

- **Beta Cats**: Play the role of the silent observer from a distance. They cautiously inch closer to see if the newcomer poses a real threat or if they might be trainable enough to fit into the existing household hierarchy.

- **Omega Cats**: I prefer a less confrontational approach. They slip into the shadows, slinking off to find a safe hiding place, perhaps hoping that this large, drooling newcomer will vanish if they don't acknowledge it.

---

1. Dr. John Bradshaw, "The Importance of Vertical Space in Cat-Dog Relationships," Feline Behavioral Studies Journal, 2019.

Each role comes with its own strategy, but the overall goal is the same: assess the threat and respond accordingly.

Dr. Karen Overall, a veterinary psychologist, suggests, "Introducing cats and dogs gradually is crucial. Start with scent swapping before any face-to-face meetings. This gives both animals time to get used to each other's presence without direct confrontation." [2]

The Slow Burn of Friendship

Cats prefer a "slow burn" approach when it comes to making friends. Their steps include:

- **Observation**: Cautious sniffing, dramatic flinching, and, most importantly, staring—long, unblinking, soul-piercing staring.

- **Testing the Waters**: The dog must prove itself worthy through consistent and respectful behaviour, not through words or gestures. Cats are watching for signs of dignity and control.

- **Setting Boundaries**: The dog must learn that the path to a cat's heart is paved with patience, calmness, and the ability to stay at least three feet away until invited otherwise.

This process is not just a test; it's an audition for the dog's ability to behave appropriately in the cat's domain.

Alpha, Beta, and Omega Roles in Friendship

The alpha cat, always the most discerning, decides if a truce is possible.

On the other hand, the beta cat is more willing to extend an olive branch, often being the first to approach the dog cautiously.

The omega cat, content to avoid conflict, observes from a safe distance, waiting until the situation is completely stable before even considering getting involved.

---

2. Dr. Karen Overall, "The Art of Gradual Introductions Between Cats and Dogs," Journal of Veterinary Psychology, 2020.

These roles determine how the cats navigate the potential friendship, each contributing differently.

Training the Dog: A Cat's Perspective

Cat Swatting at Dog During Training

Dogs often need to be taught some basic manners, and each type of cat has their own training approach:

- **Alpha Cats**: Take the lead in training, quickly establishing rules to ensure the dog knows who's boss. They use physical cues and sheer psychological warfare.

- **Beta Cats**: Are more lenient, stepping in only when absolutely necessary, but still assert their authority when needed.

- **Omega Cats**: Usually content to let the alphas do the heavy lifting, but may participate if they feel the need to defend their space.

Cats employ a combination of well-timed swats, disdainful looks, and calculated avoidance to ensure that dogs understand boundaries. Over time, the dog learns that any affection must be on the cat's terms.

Animal behaviourist Dr. Jackson Galaxy, explains, "Cats are excellent at setting boundaries. It's important for owners to respect those boundaries and intervene if the dog gets too excited. This helps build a positive relationship between the two." [3]

The Odd Couple Moments

Cat and Dog Napping Together

Despite their differences, sometimes a cat and a dog will form an odd friendship—the kind that surprises everyone. Here's how the different cats may respond:

- **Alpha Cats**: They will only share such moments if they believe the dog has earned them. It's a privilege, not a right.

- **Beta Cats**: Are more open to such arrangements, seeing the benefit of warmth and perhaps even companionship.

- **Omega Cats**: Might wait until they see that the dog can be trusted not to roll over unexpectedly, squishing them in the process.

These moments—napping together, batting tails playfully, or sharing toys—are small victories for coexistence, proof that even the most unlikely of friendships can find common ground.

When Things Get Hairy

Cat and Dog in a Chaotic Chase

Naturally, there will be disagreements. Perhaps the dog forgets the rules and chases the cat across the living room. In moments like these, the household can feel like a scene from an old slapstick comedy—furniture rattles, tails puff up, and there's a flurry of paw swipes and barks. The dog, in its excitement, may think it's all a game, while the cat sees it as an unforgivable breach of etiquette.

The alpha cat will be the first to retaliate, ensuring that boundaries are reinforced. The beta cat, while usually more diplomatic, will also step in if pushed too far. Omega cats, in contrast, will likely retreat to their hiding spots, letting the higher-ups handle the drama.

Once the dust settles, the cat will often return to its high perch, resuming its nonchalant demeanour. It might give the dog one final withering glare as if to say, "That was just a minor setback in my world domination plan." For the dog, the event is quickly forgotten—just another baffling episode in its quest for friendship. For the cat, however, it is catalogued, analyzed, and stored for future reference.

Dr. Temple Grandin advises, "When tensions rise, it's important to give both pets space. Cats, in particular, need time to regain their sense of control and security." [4]

Lessons in Diplomacy

The relationship between a cat and a dog is a study in diplomacy. The roles of each type of cat in this dynamic are crucial:

- **Alpha Cats**: Act as the household diplomat, ensuring that the dog learns lessons swiftly and effectively. They are quick to establish boundaries.

- **Beta Cats**: Are more likely to mediate, finding ways to keep the peace while maintaining their own space.

- **Omega Cats**: Observe and adapt based on the dynamics established by the alphas and betas, rarely getting directly involved but learning from the actions of the others.

Over time, as the dog learns patience and the cat grows more tolerant, these small victories accumulate, transforming the cat-dog relationship from mere coexistence into something resembling friendship.

Reflections on Cross-Species Harmony

So, when we think about cats and dogs living together, it's not just about peaceful coexistence. It's about respect, a little compromise, and a lot of patience—mostly from the cats, of course. There are no grand gestures or declarations of loyalty. Instead, it's a gradual accumulation of tiny moments: a cat choosing not to swat when the dog sniffs too close, a dog lying quietly while the cat naps nearby. And who knows? Maybe, just maybe, your alpha cat will find that the dog isn't so bad after all, even if they still think they could do without the slobber. After all, even the most regal of felines can sometimes benefit from a little unconditional love—and maybe even a slobbery kiss or two.

The Cat's Manual for Dealing with Dogs

If cats could write a manual for dealing with dogs, it would likely be filled with chapters on maintaining control, establishing boundaries, and a section devoted to "How to Train Your Dog Without Them Knowing." The alpha cat would lead with advice like: "Always maintain the high ground—both physically and metaphorically." This is followed by beta cat contributions that focus on peaceful negotiations, suggesting, "Choose the right moments to extend a paw of tolerance." And the omega cats? They'd probably recommend hiding out under the bed until it's clear that the dog isn't going anywhere.

Training isn't just for dogs, of course. Cats know that they have to train their humans as well—to set up the perfect cat-friendly environment.

A dog's introduction into the house is, for a cat, a test of their human's loyalty. Did the human set up extra perches so the cat could observe from a distance? Did they establish separate feeding stations to avoid awkward encounters? If the answer is yes, the human may earn a few points in the cat's favour.

Dr. Nicholas Dodman, recommends, "Cats need designated safe zones where dogs are not allowed. These spaces give cats a sense of security and control, which is essential for a harmonious household." [5]

How Dogs See Cats

From the dog's perspective, the cat is an enigma. They're fast, agile, and entirely uninterested in play—or at least that's how it seems. For dogs, cats are like the aloof celebrity they desperately want an autograph from. The dog thinks: "If only I could just get close enough, I know we'd be best friends!" Unfortunately, their enthusiasm often leads to blunders, like bounding up to the cat, only to receive a well-placed swat in response.

Dogs tend to live in the moment, and for them, every interaction with the cat is a fresh opportunity. Yesterday's rejection? Forgotten. Today could be the day they finally touch their noses or share a sunny spot. It's this hopeful optimism that makes dogs so endearing—and so baffling to cats, who prefer a far more measured approach to social interactions.

The Role of Humans in Feline-Canine Relations

Humans play a critical role in maintaining peace between their feline and canine companions. Setting boundaries for the dog, creating safe spaces for the cat, and providing plenty of treats during successful interactions can make all the difference. Humans need to understand that the cat-dog

---

5. Dr. Nicholas Dodman, "Creating Safe Zones for Cats in Dog-Friendly Homes," Journal of Feline Safety, 2021.

dynamic is not something to rush. Friendship cannot be forced—it has to be grown, one careful interaction at a time.

When a dog first joins the family, it's up to the human to ensure that introductions are made carefully. The cat needs places to retreat, to observe, and to determine if this new creature is a friend or foe. Meanwhile, the dog needs to learn that chasing is off-limits and that respecting the cat's boundaries will earn rewards—like praise, treats, and maybe even a tolerating look from the cat.

Training sessions that involve both the cat and the dog can help build a mutual understanding. Simple activities like feeding them treats in each other's presence, without allowing the dog to invade the cat's space, help create positive associations. The human's job is to be a mediator—a guide who ensures that both parties feel safe and secure.

The Small Steps to Peace

Ultimately, the journey to a peaceful cat-dog relationship is paved with small steps. It's in those moments when the cat lets the dog walk by without hissing, or when the dog lays down calmly as the cat eats. It's in the hesitant nose boop that finally happens one day, or in the times they share a room without incident. Over time, these small steps accumulate, and before long, you have a home where cats and dogs aren't just coexisting—they're living together in their own uniquely balanced harmony.

So, if you find yourself wondering if cats and dogs can ever truly get along, remember: it's all about the little things. A shared sunbeam, a quiet nap on opposite ends of the same couch, a tail wag met with a slow blink—these are the building blocks of cross-species friendship—a reminder that even the most different creatures can find common ground, given time, patience, and the occasional treat.

When the Hierarchy Shifts

Dealing with Changes in Rank

Cats are known for their complex social structures, and just when you think you've got everything figured out, the hierarchy can change. These shifts can happen for several reasons:

- **Addition of a New Cat**: Introducing a new member to the group can disrupt established dynamics.

- **Illness or Aging**: The illness or ageing of a current member may alter their position within the hierarchy.

- **Personality Shifts**: Changes in personality can also affect the balance among cats.

This chapter will help you navigate these changes, support your cats through transitions, and maintain a peaceful environment. By understanding these shifts, you can ensure a harmonious home, even during challenging times. Adapting effectively will prepare you to handle surprises and help your feline companions regain their balance.

Adding a New Cat to the Mix: Introducing a New Player

Adjusting to Hierarchy Shift

Behavioural Signs to Watch

Cats use subtle body language to communicate their comfort or discomfort during introductions:

- **Comfortable Signs**: A relaxed posture, ears facing forward, and slow blinking indicate that a cat is open to interaction.

- **Discomfort Signs**: Flattened ears, dilated pupils, and tense body suggest a cat feels uncomfortable.

Observing these subtle cues helps you gauge the progress of the introduction and determine when to step in or give them more space. Understanding these signals is critical to ensuring that introductions remain positive and minimal tensions, helping you build a foundation for a peaceful multi-cat household.

Dr John Bradshaw, author of *Cat Sense*, notes, "Introducing a new cat is all about patience and making sure existing cats don't feel threatened by the newcomer."[1]

New Cat, New Dynamics

Introducing a new cat into a household with established feline residents can feel like throwing a wildcard into a well-settled deck. The existing cats have their own established territories, routines, and relationships, and a newcomer can easily upset the balance. The key to a successful introduction lies in patience and careful planning. It's about managing expectations and recognizing that every cat is different—some might adjust quickly, while others will need more time and reassurance.

To better understand different perspectives, consider the approach of each type of cat:

- **Alpha Cat**: Likely to be the most territorial and wary of the newcomer. They need extra time and space to adjust and may require careful reassurance that their position in the household is not under threat.

- **Beta Cat**: More flexible and likely to approach the newcomer with curiosity. They often play the role of peacekeeper, helping ease tension between the alpha cat and the new arrival.

- **Omega Cat**: Maybe more submissive and avoidant, preferring to observe from a distance until they feel secure. They might require encouragement to interact positively with the new cat.

Think of it as a diplomatic negotiation between two dignitaries—every step must be taken carefully to ensure a peaceful outcome. Start by providing a separate space for the new cat, allowing them to adjust to the sights and smells of their new environment without direct confrontation. Gradually introduce scent-swapping by exchanging bedding or toys between the new cat and the existing one. This helps familiarize each cat

---

1. Dr. John Bradshaw, "The Importance of Vertical Space in Cat-Dog Relationships," Feline Behavioural Studies Journal, 2019.

with the other's scent, which is an important step in reducing territorial aggression.

When it's time for face-to-face meetings, keep them brief and positive:

- **Alpha Cat**: Introduce with caution and at a distance, using treats as a reward for calm behaviour.

- **Beta Cat**: Encourage gentle, supervised interactions to help build a positive association.

- **Omega Cat**: Allow them to approach at their own pace, ensuring they have a safe retreat if they feel overwhelmed.

The goal is to create positive associations with each other's presence, reinforcing the idea that the new cat is not a threat but a new family member.

Picture the alpha cat sitting on a high perch, giving the new cat a look that clearly says, "You may live here, but let's get one thing straight—I'm still the boss." Meanwhile, the beta cat casually strolls up, sniffing the new cat like they're meeting a new neighbour at a potluck, and the omega cat peeks out from behind a chair, contemplating whether this newcomer is a friend or just another one to avoid.

New Cat Introduction

Shifts Due to Aging or Illness

Changes in hierarchy can also occur when an older cat becomes less dominant due to age or illness. The alpha cat may begin to lose their status, which can lead to confusion or tension among the other cats. It's essential to closely monitor these shifts and provide additional support to the ageing or ill cat to ensure they feel secure and valued within the household.

Dr Karen Overall, a veterinary behaviourist, explains, "Older cats often need extra care when their status changes. Providing dedicated spaces for rest and retreat can help maintain their sense of security." [2]

Perspective During Shifts

- **Alpha Cat**: If the once-alpha cat is ageing or ill, it may struggle to lose dominance. Provide extra attention and ensure it still has access to its favourite spots to prevent distress.

- **Beta Cat**: The beta cat may step up to fill the leadership gap, but they often do so gently. Ensure this transition happens without too much pressure on the ageing alpha.

- **Omega Cat**: Omega cats might feel more stressed during these shifts, sensing the change in dynamics. To minimize anxiety, give them extra safe spaces and comfort.

Provide cosy resting spots that are easily accessible for older cats and ensure they have uninterrupted access to resources like food, water, and litter boxes. If a younger cat begins to take on a more dominant role, help facilitate this transition by minimizing potential conflicts. This may involve feeding the older cat separately or providing vertical spaces where they can retreat without being disturbed.

Recognizing these shifts and adjusting your approach accordingly can help maintain harmony. It's about balancing the needs of the ageing cat with

---

2. Dr. Karen Overall, "The Art of Gradual Introductions Between Cats and Dogs," Journal of Veterinary Psychology, 2020.

the dynamics of the rest of the group, ensuring everyone feels comfortable and respected.

Aging Cat in Resting Spot

Personality Shifts and the Ripple Effect

Cats' personalities can change over time due to various factors such as environment, health, or even social relationships. A once timid cat may suddenly become more assertive, or a previously dominant cat may take a backseat. These shifts can ripple through the entire household, affecting the established hierarchy.

If you notice a change in one cat's behaviour, note how it impacts the others. Increased aggression, changes in grooming habits, or shifts in where they choose to sleep can all indicate a hierarchy change. You must observe and intervene when necessary to prevent conflicts and ensure that all cats feel safe.

Dr Jackson Galaxy, a cat behaviour consultant, advises, "Changes in a cat's personality can lead to ripple effects throughout the household. Stay vigilant and ready to offer extra support during these times." [3]

Understanding Different Reactions

- **Alpha Cat**: If an alpha cat becomes more withdrawn, it can create a power vacuum. Be attentive to prevent aggressive power grabs by other cats and provide the alpha with their familiar comforts.

- **Beta Cat**: A beta cat might become more dominant if they sense the alpha cat's withdrawal. This can be a natural progression but should be managed to prevent bullying.

- **Omega Cat**: If an omega cat becomes more confident, it's a positive sign. Encourage this with interactive play, but make sure it doesn't disrupt the overall balance.

If a more timid cat begins asserting itself, provide opportunities for it to express this new confidence without causing friction. Interactive play sessions can be a great way to channel newfound assertiveness positively. Conversely, if a dominant cat becomes more withdrawn, ensure it still has access to its favourite spots and is not being pushed out by other cats.

Personality Shifts Among Cats

Emotional Well-Being and Stress Management

Changes in hierarchy can significantly affect the emotional well-being of each cat and the overall atmosphere of the household. It's crucial to know how each group member handles stress and make adjustments to improve their well-being.

Perspective on Stress Management

- **Alpha Cat**: Alpha cats often feel the most pressure to maintain their status, especially when changes occur. To alleviate their stress, provide them with high perches and exclusive spaces to retreat and feel secure. Maintaining access to favourite toys and ensuring they receive regular one-on-one interaction helps them feel valued and less anxious about maintaining their rank.

- **Beta Cat**: Beta cats may experience moderate stress, particularly if they feel they are expected to take on a more dominant role. Interactive play is an excellent way for them to channel energy positively, providing them with an outlet to express confidence. Make sure beta cats have opportunities to build self-esteem without needing to challenge the alpha directly.

- **Omega Cat**: Omega cats are the most sensitive to changes, often absorbing stress from others in the household. Offering cosy hiding spots and areas where they feel safe is vital for their emotional well-being. Omega cats need gentle encouragement to participate in group activities without pressure. Using calming pheromone sprays in their favourite spaces can also help them manage stress.

- **Human Role**: As a caregiver, you must remain observant and proactive. Monitor each cat's body language and behaviours to assess their stress levels. Providing a predictable routine for feeding, play, and affection reduces uncertainty and helps cats feel secure. Engage each cat based on their unique personality, ensuring that none feel neglected or threatened by the changes happening around them.

Dr Sarah Ellis, cat behaviour specialist, says, "Understanding each cat's unique stress triggers and providing individualized support is key to managing a harmonious multi-cat household." [4]

---

4. Dr. Sarah Ellis, "Managing Stress in Multi-Cat Households," Journal of Feline Behavior, 2021.

Tips for Managing Stress During Hierarchy Changes

- **Routine and Consistency**: Keeping feeding, play, and affection schedules consistent can help all cats feel more secure, as they will know what to expect each day.

- **Safe Spaces**: Provide multiple hiding spots and elevated areas for each cat to retreat when they need alone time. Vertical spaces, in particular, are comforting for alpha cats who need to feel in control.

- **Interactive Toys**: Use toys that stimulate a cat's natural hunting instincts to distract from hierarchy tensions. Interactive toys can help beta and omega cats build confidence and allow alpha cats to expend excess energy constructively.

Pheromone Diffusers: Consider using pheromone diffusers to create a calming environment. These products mimic natural feline pheromones, signalling safety and comfort, which is especially helpful for anxious cats like the omega.

Calm Human Energy: Cats are perceptive and can pick up on their humans' energy. Even during stressful situations, maintaining a calm demeanour can help soothe your cats. Avoid raising your voice or making sudden movements during tense moments to prevent escalating the cats' stress.

Humorous Anecdote: Imagine each cat participating in a yoga class for stress relief. The alpha cat claims the front mat, occasionally glaring at the others. The beta cat tries every pose diligently, while the omega cat is happy to find a cosy spot in the child's pose. Every cat handles stress differently, and it's your job to guide them through it!

Supporting Your Cats Through the Transition

Changes in hierarchy can be stressful for cats, so providing extra comfort and stability is crucial. Maintain consistent routines for feeding, playtime, and affection to give your cats a sense of security during times of change. Routines help reduce anxiety by providing predictability, which is especially important when social dynamics are shifting.

Dr Temple Grandin, an animal behaviour expert, says, "Cats thrive on routine, especially when dealing with social changes. Keeping feeding times consistent can greatly reduce their stress levels." [5]

Offer plenty of positive reinforcement when you see your cats interacting peacefully. Treats, praise, or extra petting can go a long way in reinforcing good behaviour and easing tensions. Additionally, ensure each cat has its own safe space where it can retreat if it feels overwhelmed. High perches, cosy hiding spots, and separate feeding areas can all help reduce stress and prevent conflicts.

In some cases, pheromone diffusers can be helpful in creating a calming environment. These products mimic natural cat pheromones that signal safety and comfort, which can be particularly useful during periods of social upheaval.

Imagine the chaos when dinner time changes by just ten minutes. The alpha cat sits by the bowl, giving you the look of ultimate betrayal; the beta cat paces nervously, and the omega cat has already decided to hide under the bed until the universe restores order. Routine really is everything!

Cats Using High Perches

Conclusion: Embracing Change

Cat hierarchies are fluid, and changes are a natural part of life in a multi-cat household. You can help your feline companions navigate these shifts with minimal stress by staying observant, patient, and proactive. Embrace the changes as they come, and remember that your role is to support each cat's well-being, ensuring they all feel secure and valued.

Whether it's introducing a new cat, supporting an ageing feline, or adapting to personality changes, your guidance can help maintain a balanced and peaceful home. Ultimately, the goal is a harmonious household where every cat feels loved and comfortable regardless of their place in the hierarchy.

Additional Considerations for a Balanced Household

- **Territorial Marking**: Cats often mark their territory through scent glands. Understanding how each cat marks territory can help you identify when conflicts are brewing. Providing extra scratch posts and areas for scent marking can ease tension.

- **Dietary Adjustments**: When hierarchies shift, dietary changes might be necessary. For example, an older cat may need softer food or a different feeding schedule than younger cats. Tailoring each cat's diet to their needs helps ensure no one feels neglected.

- **Interactive Play**: Play is an essential part of managing cat relationships. Structured play sessions with toys that mimic prey can help diffuse tension and provide an outlet for energy that might otherwise be directed toward conflict.

- **Observation and Record Keeping**: Record significant behavioural changes. A journal noting which cat displays certain behaviours, such as aggressive grooming or guarding resources, can be invaluable in understanding and managing changes in hierarchy. This can help you identify patterns and adjust your approach accordingly.

- **Introducing Comfort Objects**: Sometimes, providing a comfort object like a favourite toy or blanket can make transitions easier for cats. These objects can offer familiarity, reducing stress during interactions with other cats.

Picture the omega cat finally mustering the courage to jump onto a high perch, only to find the alpha cat staring them down with an expression that says, "Nice try, rookie." Cats may be complex, but their determination to maintain—or challenge—their position in the household never gets old!

Leadership in the Feline World

Beyond the Alpha

Rethinking Feline Leadership

The idea of the "alpha, beta, and omega" framework has long influenced how we perceive feline social structures, but let's face it: cats have never been known to follow anyone else's rules, let alone a strict hierarchy. In this chapter, we will dispel the myths surrounding feline leadership and explore what it really means to be in charge in a world where the line between leader and follower is often blurred. Cats don't follow the pack mentality often attributed to them. Instead, they form intricate social structures that are more fluid and dynamic than rigid hierarchies. Understanding these complex dynamics is key to maintaining peace and stability in your multi-cat household.

Let's get beyond the stereotypes and embrace the delightful complexity of feline leadership.

Cats are independent, mysterious creatures, and the concept of alpha, beta, and omega roles better captures the nuances of their social dynamics. Alpha cats might take the lead, but beta and omega cats contribute uniquely to group harmony.

While some cats might naturally take on a leadership role, it's not about dominance as it might be for pack animals. Cats lead in subtle, varied ways—sometimes through quiet confidence, other times through nurturing gestures or playful charm. The beauty of feline social structures lies in their fluidity.

- **Fluid Roles**: Cats don't need a strict chain of command; they have their own intricate ways of establishing roles, which often change depending on the situation.

    - One day, a cat might be the ruler of the highest perch.

    - The next day, they might step aside for another to take that spot.

    - They adapt based on mood, health, or group dynamics.

- **Observation and Patience**: This constant ebb and flow makes living with multiple cats an exercise in observation, patience, and a bit of humour.

    - Watching these interactions can teach valuable lessons about the flexibility of leadership.

    - Sometimes, simply observing without interfering is the best way to help maintain harmony.

Understanding these complex dynamics is essential if you want to keep the peace in a multi-cat household. It's about recognizing that cats don't like to be boxed into any role—least of all that of a predictable, regimented follower. Leadership among cats is far more intricate and interesting than any simple alpha-beta structure. Each cat contributes in its own way, whether by leading, following, nurturing, or simply providing a calming presence.

- **Supporting Each Role**: Each role within the group contributes to the overall harmony. Understanding how to nurture each type of role is important so every cat feels valued.

  - **Alpha Cats**: Need reassurance of their status without unnecessary challenges.

  - **Beta Cats**: Benefit from opportunities to mediate and show leadership when the alpha cat takes a step back.

  - **Omega Cats**: Thrive when provided with comfort and stability, contributing quietly to group dynamics.

Let's explore the many faces of feline leadership, from the charismatic peacekeeper to the quiet nurturer, and learn how humans can support and foster a healthy environment where every cat finds their place.

- **Human Involvement**: Knowing when and how to support these different roles is crucial for a balanced household. Providing resources and creating an environment where leadership can shift without conflict is key.

The Different Roles Within a Feline Group

Cats in Various Roles

The Alpha and Beyond: The Many Roles of Feline Leadership

The concept of the "alpha" might resonate well with wolves, but it's not always straightforward for cats.

- **Shared Responsibilities**: Cats often share responsibilities, and leadership can shift depending on circumstances.

  - There might be a confident explorer, a peacekeeper, or a self-appointed chief nap inspector.

  - Each cat has strengths that allow it to take on different roles at different times, ensuring a balanced dynamic.

- **Flexible Roles**: Recognizing these varied roles helps us understand that every cat contributes to the household in their own way.

  - **Alpha Cats**: Typically take the lead, managing territory and ensuring access to resources.

  - **Beta Cats**: Often support the alpha, playing the role of peacekeeper and maintaining social harmony.

  - **Omega Cats**: Provide a calming presence, avoid conflict, and offer emotional support by being content and calm.

Cats don't adhere to the rigid hierarchies that many other animals do. Instead, the roles of alpha, beta, and omega in feline groups are fluid, adapting based on each cat's personality, strengths, and the specific circumstances within the group. Their social roles are flexible, with each cat sometimes stepping into leadership based on their strengths, the situation, or even just their mood.

- **Adaptable Leadership**:

  - Some cats take charge during mealtimes.

  - Others prefer to lead during play.

○ Others bask in the warmth of camaraderie.

- **No Strict Rank**: The heart of feline leadership is its adaptability, accommodating different personalities and needs without demanding strict adherence to rank.

  ○ This flexibility is what makes feline groups resilient, as roles can change depending on the group's needs.

Caregivers and Mediators: The Beta and Omega Roles

The Caregiver Cat

The Caregiver Cat

The caregiving role is often overlooked, but it plays a huge part in the stability of feline groups. This role is typically more aligned with beta or omega cats, who provide nurturing support and help maintain social bonds within the group. This cat might not be the alpha, but they helps nurture the social bond by grooming others or curling up to comfort a stressed cat.

- **Strengthening Relationships**: Dr Sarah Ellis points out that caregiving helps strengthen relationships and lowers stress levels in the group.[1]

---

1. Dr. Sarah Ellis, *Feline Behavior and Social Dynamics*, Journal of Feline Studies, 2020.

- ○ Grooming a friend.

- ○ Curling up to comfort another cat when things get tense.

- **Quiet Leadership**: Caregivers foster a nurturing environment crucial for group stability.

  - ○ Grooming.

  - ○ Sharing warmth.

  - ○ Acting as a buffer during conflicts.

- **Reducing Stress**: Imagine a cat instinctively curling up next to another who's anxious or under the weather—this act alone can significantly reduce stress and solidify social bonds.

Their quiet leadership through care is what helps maintain balance and unity among the cats.

- **Emotional Needs of Caregivers**: Beta and omega cats who take on caregiving roles also need human reassurance and support. Providing positive reinforcement during these nurturing moments helps them continue their essential role within the group.

Leadership Dynamics in a Multi-Cat Household

Shifting Leadership Roles

Leadership Shifts Over Time

Leadership isn't set in stone; cats might change roles depending on age, health, or even mood. Alpha cats may become more passive as they age, allowing beta cats to take on more prominent roles, while omega cats can sometimes step up to support others during times of change.

- **Constant Change**: This constant ebb and flow keeps things interesting and, sometimes, a bit chaotic.

  - An ageing alpha steps down.

  - A younger cat steps up.

  - A timid cat grows bolder.

- **Natural Shifts**: Changes in leadership dynamics are often so subtle that they go unnoticed until suddenly, one cat takes over as the "king of the couch" while the former leader takes a backseat.

  - These natural transitions are typically smooth, but humans should observe them and provide support as needed.

- **Observation is Key**: The key is observing these changes without trying to enforce a particular order; cats are remarkably good at figuring things out themselves, even if they seem chaotic.

  - Understanding when to step in and when to step back is crucial for maintaining group harmony.

Signs of Leadership Shift

*Recognizing Leadership
Changes*

How do you know when the leadership is shifting?

- **Changes in Grooming Behavior**: An older cat that used to groom others might now be on the receiving end, signalling its acceptance of a more submissive role. This shift can affect each type of cat differently—an alpha cat may become less dominant, a beta cat might step up to lead, and an omega cat may become more involved in social activities.

    ○ Grooming is often a social signal that indicates changing dynamics.

- **Access to Resources**:

    ○ Changes in who has access to prime napping spots.

    ○ Changes in who eats first from the food bowls.

    ○ These changes are subtle yet significant indicators of shifting roles.

- **Conflict Resolution**:

    ○ Pay attention to who steps in to mediate conflicts or guide group activities.

○ Leadership shifts might also be evident in resolving conflicts—who steps in to diffuse a tense situation?

○ The cat that steps up during conflicts often becomes a new leader in some aspects of the group dynamic.

As a cat owner, staying attuned to these signs can help you support your cats during their transitions, making the shifts as smooth as possible for everyone.

Maintaining Harmony During Leadership Changes

Sharing Resources to
Maintain Harmony

During times of leadership change, the household can become unsettled. It's important to create a stable environment by providing multiple resources—food, water, litter boxes, and cosy resting places—so that no one feels deprived.

- **Reduce Competition**: As Dr John Bradshaw, a renowned feline behaviour expert, suggests, reducing competition for resources is one of the best ways to ease tensions during these periods of change. [2]

  ○ Adding extra resources can make all the difference in reducing

2. Dr. John Bradshaw, *Understanding Feline Social Hierarchies*, Feline Behavioral Insights, 2019.

friction between cats.

- **Ensure Plenty of Resources**:

  - Multiple food bowls.

  - Multiple litter boxes.

  - Cosy resting spots.

  - Providing plenty of each essential resource helps ensure that each cat can find their own space when needed.

- **Avoiding Conflict**: Adding extra bowls, boxes, and cosy spots ensures that no cat feels like they have to compete for essentials, helping prevent conflict before it starts.

  - Conflict prevention is key to maintaining harmony during transitional phases.

Maintaining a calm environment with plenty of resources is the secret to a peaceful transition.

The Role of Human Support During Leadership Changes

*Human Support During
Transitions*

Knowing When to Step In

Supporting leadership changes is different from simply managing conflict. It's about knowing when a shift is happening and how to assist without interfering too much. Cats can work out a lot on their own, but as their human, you play an important role in keeping the peace.

- **Observe Reactions**: If you notice that a younger cat is beginning to take over a leadership role from an older cat, observe how the other cats are reacting.

  - Are they accepting the change?

  - Is there tension brewing?

- **Provide Support**: Your role is to provide support by offering comfort to the older cat while reinforcing positive behaviour in the younger cat.

  - Providing treats during peaceful moments to encourage a smooth transition.

  - Positive reinforcement can make a significant difference in how smoothly the transition goes.

- **Human as Mediator**: Sometimes, humans must act as mediators to ensure no cat feels threatened or left out during a shift.

  - Gentle intervention can help prevent disputes and ease tensions.

Think of yourself as a coach on the sidelines—ready to step in when necessary, but mostly to observe and cheer them on. You don't need to control every interaction, but you must ensure that no one is unfairly sidelined. This kind of balanced intervention can help facilitate a peaceful shift in leadership without creating additional stress for your feline companions.

Offering Additional Support

During leadership changes, it's not just about managing behaviour—it's also about providing emotional support, which can vary based on the cat's role. Alpha cats may need reassurance that they are still valued, beta cats might benefit from encouragement as they take on new responsibilities, and omega cats often need extra comfort to feel secure during changes.

- **Spend Extra Time**: Cats are sensitive to change, and a shifting social dynamic can be stressful for everyone involved.

  - Playtime.

  - Grooming.

  - Sitting nearby.

- **Emotional Support**: Emotional support is key to helping all cats adjust to new roles, whether stepping up or down.

Conclusion: Beyond the Alpha - Embracing Fluid Leadership

Different Behaviours

The concept of leadership in the feline world goes far beyond the traditional idea of the alpha. Cats exhibit various leadership behaviours, from nurturing caregivers to empathetic leaders like Jonah. The key to maintaining a harmonious multi-cat household is understanding that these roles are fluid and adaptable.

- **Observe and Reinforce**: By observing your cats' behaviours, reinforcing positive leadership, and providing support during transitions, you can help create a balanced and peaceful home where every cat feels valued and secure, regardless of their role.

So the next time you see your cats in action, remember—they may not have a strict leader, but they have their own unique system that works just fine for them. Whether they're grooming each other, vying for the best perch, or quietly mediating between others, each role is vital to the social fabric of your feline family. Embrace the diversity of their personalities, celebrate the shifts in leadership, and enjoy the wonderful, ever-changing dynamics of your cats' world. Every cat, from the confident alpha to the nurturing omega, plays an irreplaceable part in the household, and this balance creates a thriving, happy environment for all.

Creating an Ideal Environment

for Social Harmony

Designing the Perfect Feline Kingdom

Every cat owner dreams of a household where harmony reigns and all feline companions coexist peacefully. While that may sound like a fairy tale when you're breaking up the latest standoff over the prime sunny spot, creating an environment that promotes social harmony is more than possible—it's an art.

Just like a royal architect designing a palace for some finicky monarchs, you need to plan every detail with feline preferences in mind. From strategically placed litter boxes to perfectly chosen napping perches, a well-thought-out environment can make all the difference in ensuring your cats feel comfortable, respected, and blissfully content. Let's dive into the details of crafting a feline-friendly household that is as harmonious as it is fit for royalty.

Space: It's All About Territory

Ensuring each cat has their own space is key to a harmonious multi-cat household. Cats are territorial creatures, and ensuring everyone has their own little corner of the kingdom can help avoid conflicts. Think of it as creating mini-fiefdoms for your four-legged royalty—each cat needs a piece of real estate entirely their own.

Highways and Byways

Cats like to move about the house in specific pathways, often called "cat highways." If these routes intersect too often, it can create friction between the residents. Your goal is to create an environment with multiple routes around the house. This allows each cat to travel without constantly bumping into another. Wall shelves, perches, or even strategically placed furniture can help achieve this. This way, they can hold their heads high and strut their stuff without feeling like they're running a gauntlet. Think of it as adding extra lanes to avoid traffic jams during rush hour.

Elevated Spaces

Cats love to be up high. Giving them access to elevated spaces like cat trees, wall shelves, or even the top of a bookshelf can reduce conflicts by allowing a cat to distance itself from others when needed physically. According to Dr Sarah Heath, a veterinary behaviourist, the vertical territory is one of the most effective ways to reduce anxiety and maintain harmony in a multi-cat household. Elevated spaces provide cats with a sense of control and security by allowing them to observe their surroundings from a safe vantage point, which helps to reduce feelings of vulnerability and stress.[1] By providing plenty of elevated spots, you ensure that even the shyest or most anxious cat has a safe place to observe from above—a regal throne, if you will, far from the hustle and bustle below.

Resources: The More, The Merrier

Litter Boxes, Food, and Water

One of the easiest ways to create a peaceful environment is to ensure there are enough resources to go around. This means multiple litter boxes, food bowls, and water stations, ideally spread throughout different areas of the house. The golden rule here is one per cat plus an extra. This way, no cat feels the need to guard or defend their resources. After all, nothing sparks a feud quite like a lack of essential supplies—it's the equivalent of running out of snacks at a royal banquet.

The Resource Allocation Plan

Comfortable Retreats: The Importance of Privacy

Cats need space, not only from each other but from the bustling activities of human life. Just like we need an occasional break from social interaction, cats need quiet, private spots where they can rest undisturbed.

Creating cosy retreats for each cat—whether a box tucked under a bed, a sunny windowsill, or a plush cave bed—gives them a place to retreat when

---

1. Dr. Sarah Heath, *Feline Behavioral Health and Welfare*, Elsevier, 2015.

they need some downtime. These little hideaways are perfect for when even the most sociable cat needs a break from their royal subjects.

Choosing the Perfect Spot

Selecting where to place these cosy retreats is half the battle. Make sure each cat has a few options—elevated spots, hidden corners, or sunny spots near windows—so they can choose depending on their mood. Cats are a bit like introverted extroverts; sometimes, they want to watch from a safe distance, and others want to be in the middle. Respecting their choice of where to rest helps reduce the chances of conflict. And who could blame them? Even the Queen sometimes needs a break from her royal duties.

Interactive Tip for Readers: Spend a few days observing your cats' behaviour to determine their favourite spots. Once you have an idea, create retreats in those areas to cater to their preferences. You might find that adding a soft blanket or moving a chair closer to a sunny window can make all the difference in their comfort.

Encouraging Positive Social Interaction

Play: The Great Social Equalizer

One of the best ways to foster positive relationships between your cats is through play. Interactive toys like wand teasers, laser pointers, or even a good ol' cardboard box can work wonders in redirecting any pent-up energy into fun rather than feuds. A group play session, where everyone gets a turn, helps reduce jealousy and gives the cats a sense of camaraderie. Think of it as organizing a royal tournament where everyone gets to compete without anyone losing their crown.

According to Dr Sophia Yin, interactive play is crucial for helping cats bond. It allows them to engage in positive activities together rather than competing for territory or resources. Play also mimics hunting behaviours, which helps satisfy their instincts, reducing tension and anxiety within the group.[2]

Rewarding the Good Stuff

Cats are more likely to repeat behaviours that are positively reinforced. Treats, praise, or a favourite toy can go a long way in encouraging peaceful coexistence. For example, if your cats share a space without hissing or growling, give them a treat or give a gentle head rub as a reward. According to cat behaviourist Jackson Galaxy, positive reinforcement can help make desired behaviours stick, eventually fostering a more peaceful household.[3] Remember, each cat needs its own reward—because nothing says "war" quite like sharing a single snack.

Imagine if you had to share your dessert every time you did something right. Chaos! Cats feel the same way—reward them individually, and you'll keep the peace.

Treat Time Diplomacy

Enrichment: Keeping Minds Active

Cats are naturally curious and need mental stimulation to stay happy and avoid boredom. Bored cats can become frustrated, which may lead to conflicts. Adding cat trees, scratching posts, puzzle toys like

---

2. Dr. Sophia Yin, *The Good Cat Behavior Guide*, CattleDog Publishing, 2013.

3. Jackson Galaxy, *Total Cat Mojo: The Ultimate Guide to Life with Your Cat*, Penguin Publishing Group, 2017.

treat-dispensing balls, and tunnels can keep them entertained and give them a healthy outlet for their natural instincts. A cardboard scratching post or a puzzle feeder with hidden treats is a great way to keep their minds engaged. Remember, a mentally stimulated cat is a content cat, and a content cat is far less likely to pick a fight over the best nap spot.

DIY Enrichment Ideas: You don't need to spend a fortune on fancy cat toys. Try creating simple enrichment items, like cardboard box mazes or homemade puzzle feeders made from toilet paper rolls. Rotating toys and creating new challenges every few weeks can keep your cats' minds engaged and reduce boredom. By keeping the environment dynamic, you're ensuring that their kingdom remains exciting and full of adventures.

Rotating Toys

One trick to keep things fresh is rotating their toys every few weeks. This prevents boredom and keeps the environment dynamic. Imagine reading the same book daily—you'd get bored, too! By keeping their environment novel, you're enriching their lives and reducing the chances of boredom-induced spats.

Dr Sarah Ellis suggests that rotating toys mimic the ever-changing stimuli of a cat's natural environment, keeping their brains active and reducing stress levels. This change in stimuli is vital for mental health, especially in multi-cat households, where tension can easily escalate if boredom sets in.[4]

Emotional Needs: Providing Comfort and Security

Creating an ideal environment for social harmony goes beyond physical resources; it also involves tending to your cats' emotional needs. Emotional security comes from spending one-on-one time with each cat, respecting their need for privacy, and recognizing when they need extra reassurance. Whether it's a grooming session, a cuddle, or just sitting quietly nearby, these moments help solidify the bond between you and your cats.

One-on-One Time

Cats, like people, value individualized attention. Spend quality time with each of your cats—play their favourite game, groom them, or let them sit on your lap while you read. These interactions are crucial for reinforcing their bond with you and helping them feel secure in their place within the household. It's the royal equivalent of private counsel with each court member—every cat deserves their moment to feel special and loved.

Think of your cats as minor royals—they may not be king or queen, but they still expect (and deserve) an audience with their human. Make time for each of them, and you'll find they're much happier to share the throne room.

Conclusion: The Royal Blueprint for Peace

Creating an ideal environment for social harmony isn't about controlling your cats—it's about understanding their needs and designing a space that respects them. You can foster a peaceful coexistence among your cats with multiple cosy spots, plenty of elevated spaces, and enough resources to go around. Remember, every cat is different—some are outgoing, others more reserved. By catering to their individual preferences and providing enough opportunities for play, enrichment, and privacy, you can build a kingdom where all your feline subjects live in harmony.

Think of yourself as the royal architect of a feline utopia. Planning carefully and observing your cats' behaviour allows you to create a space where even the most independent or anxious cat feels secure. With patience, understanding, and maybe a touch of catnip diplomacy, your household can be one where every cat finds their place, and peace truly reigns supreme.

The Ultimate Guide to Keeping the Peace

Among Feline Roommates

Feline Leadership Transitions: Navigating Multi-Cat Hierarchies

With their complex social hierarchies, cats can bring harmony and chaos into a home—like a furry sitcom where each cat plays a unique role in the drama. Understanding the changing roles of alpha, beta, and omega cats requires knowledge about feline behaviour, patience in dealing with shifting dynamics, and treats as positive reinforcement. This chapter is your ultimate guide to navigating these interactions effectively, focusing on how humans can keep the peace during these feline leadership transitions.

Understanding and Recognizing Leadership Shifts

In multi-cat households, leadership roles among alpha, beta, and omega cats are as fluid as the contents of a spilt water bowl. These roles can shift due to health, age, or the introduction of a new household member.

This often leads to dramatic changes in the social dynamic. For example, a formerly dominant cat might suddenly find themselves yielding to a newcomer.

These shifts can be both fascinating and amusing:

- Your alpha cat, once the proud ruler of the highest perch, now suddenly allows the new kitten to steal their spot, all while giving you an incredulous look as if to say, "Do you see what I have to put up with?"

- The beta cat, who was always second-in-command, may find newfound confidence and start asserting themselves in ways you never expected.

- Meanwhile, the omega cat, typically the most submissive, might take advantage of the chaos to enjoy some new privileges, like sneaking into the best sunlit spot.

Common Reasons for Leadership Shifts

- **Age or Health Changes**: An ageing alpha may start slowing down, creating an opening for a beta to move up the ranks. It's like an ageing monarch passing the crown but with fewer royal decrees and a lot more napping.

  - **Signs to Watch For**: The alpha may be less inclined to participate in high-energy activities or may start retreating from confrontations they previously would have dominated. Look for changes in their grooming habits, eating patterns, or preferred resting spots.

  - **How to Help**: Provide your ageing alpha with comfortable and exclusive resting spots, such as elevated beds that are easy to access. Maintain their routines as much as possible to give them a sense of stability. Offer special attention and gentle play to keep them engaged and content.

- **New Household Members**: Bringing in a new cat is like introducing a wildcard contestant to an ongoing reality show—it shakes everything up. The newcomer needs time to find their place, and the established hierarchy may adjust to accommodate.

  - **Scent Integration**: Use scent swapping to introduce the new cat's scent to the existing members without any visual confrontation. Rub a cloth on the newcomer and allow your existing cats to sniff it to familiarize themselves with the new scent non-threateningly.

  - **Gradual Introductions**: Introduce the new cat slowly by allowing them to explore a separate room. Feed the cats on either side of a closed door to associate the scent of the newcomer with positive experiences, like food.

  - **Supervised Play**: Gradually bring the new cat into supervised play sessions with the other cats to foster positive interactions. Keep sessions short at first and gradually increase the time as the cats grow more comfortable with one another.

- **Changes in Behavior**: Shifts in grooming habits, resource control, or mediation during conflicts are often signs that someone is trying to move up—or down—the feline ladder. Recognizing these changes can make all the difference in keeping your cat's household harmonious.

  - **Mediation Behavior**: When a beta cat starts stepping in to mediate minor squabbles between other cats, this may indicate an attempt to assert themselves as the new leader. Observing who initiates grooming sessions can also offer clues about changing dynamics.

  - **Changes in Resting Spots**: Pay attention to who takes over high-status resting spots like the top of the cat tree. These shifts can signal changes in the social hierarchy.

By closely observing these changes, you can better understand your cats' needs and adjust your approach to provide effective support during these transitions.

Real-world Scenarios of Leadership Shifts

Leadership shifts can bring unexpected challenges. It often feels like managing a small kingdom with shifting loyalties. These transitions are not always straightforward.

Each scenario can bring unique opportunities for growth—both for your cats and for you as a cat owner. Here are some common scenarios and how to handle them:

Scenario 1: Aging Alpha Becomes Submissive

What Happens: An older alpha cat may start showing signs of slowing down—retreating from confrontations or spending more time in their favourite sunlit spot. You might notice them allowing other cats to take the lead during mealtime or grooming, which can indicate they are becoming more comfortable with stepping back.

Human Response:

- **Encourage the Aging Alpha**:

  - Provide consistent access to their favourite resting spots or high perches, which still signal their status.

  - Use puzzle toys to keep them mentally stimulated without requiring too much physical effort.

- Engage in gentle play sessions to help them stay active and engaged.

  - Offer special one-on-one time to reassure them that they are still valued.

- **Support for the Beta Cat**:

  - Offer positive reinforcement, like treats or praise, when the beta cat demonstrates assertiveness without aggression. This helps solidify their role in a way that fosters harmony. (Smith, 2021) [1]

  - Introduce activities that allow the beta cat to practice leadership, such as initiating group play sessions or being the first to receive treats.

Aging Alpha: Passing the Crown

Scenario 2: Introducing a New Cat

What Happens: A new cat entering the household can shake up the established social order. It's like adding a new character to an ensemble sitcom—leaving everyone unsure if they're the hero or the villain. The

---

1. Dr. Karen Smith, Introducing New Cats into Multi-Cat Households, Journal of Feline Integration, 2021.

current alpha may feel the need to reassert their dominance, while beta and omega cats may either retreat or attempt to figure out where they now stand.

Human Response:

- **Introduce the New Cat Gradually:**

  - Use scent swapping to familiarize everyone without triggering a confrontation.

  - Ensure the new cat has a safe space where they can settle in without feeling pressured.

  - Supervise early interactions and reward positive behaviour with treats.

- **Observe Cat Reactions:**

  - Keep an eye on how the existing cats react—omegas might hide, and the alpha might act like they've got something to prove.

  - Take note of any cats attempting to avoid the newcomer, as they may need more time to adjust.

- **Provide Play Sessions:**

  - Provide interactive play sessions that involve all cats to help dissipate tension. Make sure all cats have their comfort zones intact to help everyone find their place without unnecessary drama. For example, have designated "getaway" areas for each cat so they know they can escape if interactions become too stressful. (Brown, 2022) [2]

  - Use interactive toys like feather wands or laser pointers to distract from direct confrontations and channel energy into

---

2. Dr. Lisa Brown, Calming Strategies for Omega Cats, Feline Well-being Journal, 2022.

positive play.

*New Cat Introductions: Meeting
the Cast*

Human Strategies During Leadership Shifts

When leadership roles shift, it's time for the humans to put on their referee stripes. Your involvement can ease tensions and support new dynamics. It's like managing a very fluffy corporate restructuring.

Some cats will need extra support, while others will just need a quiet corner to avoid the chaos. Here are some effective strategies to ensure a smooth transition:

- **Create Temporary Comfort Zones**: Set up designated areas for omega cats to retreat to when things get a little too 'Game of Thrones.' These safe spaces help maintain stability for those who prefer to avoid conflict and chill. Adding cosy blankets, familiar toys, and even a box or two can provide a sense of security for omegas who need time away from the spotlight. It's important for these spaces to be quiet and away from high-traffic areas of your home to offer respite truly.

  - **Enrichment in Comfort Zones**: Include calming elements like pheromone diffusers, familiar bedding, and soft music to help create a comforting retreat for stressed cats.

- **Adjust Interaction Routines**:

  - **Previous Alpha**: Give extra attention to the previous

alpha—perhaps they now need reassurance more than anything else. Spend quality time grooming, petting, or simply sitting with them.

- ○ **New Leader**: Show some extra love to the new leader to ensure they don't feel like an impostor in their new position. Help them build confidence by allowing them to lead feeding times or play sessions.

- ○ For instance, you might spend extra one-on-one time grooming or playing with the former alpha to help them relax into their new, less demanding role. Meanwhile, ensure the new alpha gets chances to lead group activities, like playtime or even leading the 'parade' to the feeding area.

- ○ **Maintain Routine**: Cats thrive on routine, so even during shifts, try to maintain feeding schedules, playtimes, and quiet times to give all cats a sense of security.

- **Targeted Play Sessions**: Playtime is an excellent way to reduce tension and manage hierarchy shifts. Use interactive toys to involve all cats, but especially focus on encouraging betas and omegas. Play sessions are like feline team-building exercises—except they actually work. Wand toys and laser pointers can help redirect any territorial energy into a fun, constructive outlet. Involve the new leader by letting them 'hunt' first while the others watch, reinforcing their new role without causing unnecessary conflict. (Thompson, 2021). [3]

- ○ **Interactive Toys**: Consider using puzzle feeders or motorized toys that encourage collaborative play, allowing cats to take turns while also building their confidence.

- **Example Play Strategy**: Set up wand toy sessions where the beta cat can 'chase' and 'catch' the toy in front of the alpha. It's like watching a sports tryout, with the alpha on the sidelines

---

3. Dr. Laura Thompson, The Role of Play in Feline Social Structures, Journal of Animal Play Studies, 2021.

giving subtle nods of approval. To make things more engaging, switch roles during play to allow each cat to build confidence in a different capacity.

- ○ **Incorporate Treats**: After play, reward each cat with a treat for participating. This reinforces positive behaviour and makes the experience enjoyable for everyone.

Feline Team Building: Playtime
Hierarchies

Building Trust and Addressing Emotional Needs

Building trust during leadership changes is key to ensuring a smooth transition. Cats need consistent relationships—especially when their social order feels like it's flipping upside down. Here's how to help each type of cat adjust during these changes:

- **Alpha Cats**: Reinforce their leadership by maintaining exclusive spots—like the top perch on the cat tree—so they still feel they've got their throne. They must know they're still the boss, even if their workload has lightened. Providing special privileges like being the first to receive treats can help reinforce their confidence during times of change. (Ellis, 2020) [4]

  - ○ **Reaffirm Confidence**: Encourage the alpha cat with grooming sessions or quiet bonding time. Reinforcing their

---

4. Dr. Sarah Ellis, Feline Behavior and Social Dynamics, Journal of Feline Studies, 2020

bond with you can provide comfort and stability during the shift.

- **Beta Cats**: Encourage beta cats to take on more group activities. Think of them as the new assistant manager—they need some responsibilities to feel confident. When they successfully mediate with other cats, positive reinforcement helps them understand their new role. Offer treats or a favourite toy when the beta cat steps in to keep the peace without causing trouble. (Bradshaw, 2019) [5]

- **Opportunities for Leadership**: Allow the beta cat to take the lead in interactive play sessions or be the first to explore new toys. This will help them adjust and accept their new responsibilities.

- **Omega Cats**: Omegas thrive on stability. They're the peaceful yoga enthusiasts of the group who just want a little consistency. Use pheromone diffusers or create cosy corners for them to help ease anxiety during any upheaval.

  - **Spend Extra Time with Omegas**: Sit with omega cats, offering gentle pets and reassurance.

  - **Provide Calming Rituals**: These calming rituals can help them stay balanced when everything else seems uncertain. (Green, 2021) [6]

  - **Pheromone Diffusers**: Use pheromone diffusers like Feliway to create a calming environment that helps omega cats feel more secure during periods of social change.

  - **Structured Routine**: Omegas benefit greatly from a structured daily routine, so keep feeding and playtimes as predictable as possible to help them feel safe.

---

5. Dr. John Bradshaw, Understanding Feline Social Hierarchies, Feline Behavioral Insights, 2019.

6. Dr. Rebecca Green, Omega Cats and Household Harmony, Feline Journal, 2021.

Trust-building techniques like clicker training, scent swapping, and positive reinforcement can ease transitions for all cats. For instance, using scent swapping between cats can reduce tension by familiarizing them with each other's scents in a non-threatening way.

Practice clicker training with omega cats to help them gain confidence. Reward small positive behaviours, such as approaching the alpha cat without fear, to reinforce a sense of accomplishment and build trust between different roles.

*Building Trust: Steps to
Emotional Security*

Acting as a Mediator

Humans are like the peacekeepers in a fluffy, occasionally hissy United Nations. Your role is to step in gently to keep the chaos from escalating into a full-blown feline standoff. It's all about reading the room (or the cat tree) and knowing when to let things play out versus when to intervene.

- **Stepping In at the Right Time**: Intervene when conflicts arise, but do it with finesse. Distracting two cats vying for the same spot with treats in separate areas is often enough to avoid a confrontation. Think of yourself as the 'household manager' whose job is to ensure everyone plays nice without stepping on any furry toes. Try using food puzzles or treat-dispensing toys as a distraction when tensions rise—it gives them something else to focus on and turns a potentially negative interaction into a rewarding experience.

  - **Use of Treat-Dispensing Toys**: These toys can serve as both a distraction and a positive reinforcement tool, providing an enjoyable activity during potentially tense moments.

- **The Humor in Chaos**: Leadership shifts can feel like a soap opera—one day, someone's in charge, and the next, they're a background character. Embrace the unpredictability. Imagine yourself as the 'sitcom director,' making sure the drama stays light and entertaining without getting out of hand. Sometimes, the best way to keep the peace is to have a sense of humour about it. After all, if your cats are treating their daily lives like an over-the-top drama, it's probably best to laugh along with them rather than stress.

  - **Stay Light-Hearted**: Maintaining a positive attitude can help your cats stay calm. They are highly perceptive and can pick up on your stress, so try to keep interactions playful and light-hearted

Transition Checklist for Leadership Changes

To help keep track of how well your cats are adjusting during leadership transitions, use this checklist:

- **Observe Grooming Changes**: Is the previous alpha still grooming others, or are they now being groomed? Changes in grooming dynamics are often a clear sign of shifting roles.

- **Monitor Resource Use**: Who can access key areas like high perches or favourite resting spots? Notice if a lower-ranked cat starts taking over prime spaces, which may indicate a shift in the hierarchy.

- **Track Conflicts and Mediation**: Who steps in to mediate or stop conflict? Are lower-ranked cats showing increased assertiveness? These observations can help identify which roles are changing and how well the new dynamics are being established.

- **Record Feeding Behavior**: Observe which cat approaches the food bowls first. A shift in feeding behaviour can also indicate a change in social rank. Ensure all cats have access to food without being bullied away.

- **Play and Interaction Levels**: Note changes in play dynamics—who initiates play and who seems more reluctant. Changes in these behaviours can signal shifts in confidence or hierarchy.

- **Emotional Well-being**: Watch for signs of stress, such as over-grooming, hiding, or a decrease in appetite. Addressing these signs early can prevent bigger problems down the line.

Using this checklist can help you understand the social dynamics at play and take appropriate action to support your cats during these changes.

Tracking Changes: The Leadership Checklist

Conclusion: Beyond the Alpha - Embracing Fluid Leadership

Embracing Feline Diversity in Leadership

The concept of leadership in the feline world goes far beyond the traditional idea of the alpha. Cats exhibit various leadership behaviours, from nurturing caregivers to empathetic leaders. The key to maintaining a harmonious multi-cat household is understanding that these roles are fluid and adaptable.

Observe and Reinforce: By observing your cats' behaviours, reinforcing positive leadership, and providing support during transitions, you can help create a balanced and peaceful home where every cat feels valued and secure, regardless of their role.

So the next time you see your cats in action, remember—they may not have a strict leader, but they have their own unique system that works just fine for them. Whether they're grooming each other, vying for the best perch, or quietly mediating between others, each role is vital to the social fabric of your feline family. Embrace the complexity, celebrate the different roles—whether alpha, beta, or omega—and enjoy the unique ways your cats lead and interact with each other and with you.

The Feline Social Symphony

Navigating Dynamics, Drama, and Harmony

The Joy of Cat-archy: Finding the Humor and Beauty in Feline Social Dynamics

Are you a proud cat owner constantly amused by the quirky social dynamics of your feline friends? If so, welcome to the club! This subchapter will explore the joy of cat-archy and how to find humour and beauty in your household's sometimes chaotic world of feline social hierarchy.

One of the most entertaining aspects of living with cats is watching them establish their rank within the home. Each cat brings a unique personality to the social mix, whether it takes on the role of a confident leader, a sneaky troublemaker, or a peacekeeper. Observing these dynamics provides endless entertainment and insight into cats' complex social lives.

- **Confident Leader**: Some cats will claim the highest perch, always surveying their surroundings with an air of authority.

- **Sneaky Trouble-Maker**: Others might sneak around and steal prime spots from their fellow felines, keeping everyone on their toes.

- **Peacekeeper**: Some also step in to diffuse tensions, ensuring everyone plays nicely and maintains balance.

These individual quirks add flavour to the household dynamic. Every day is unpredictable and entertaining, filled with drama, comedy, and plenty of unexpected plot twists. As your cats interact, challenge each other, and occasionally team up for a common goal—usually involving food or a particularly elusive toy—you get a front-row seat to a never-ending show.

The beauty of feline social dynamics lies in the bonds that form over time. Cats can form strong, enduring relationships with their fellow feline housemates, often engaging in playful antics and affectionate grooming sessions that warm the heart.

It's not uncommon to see two cats who were once fierce rivals become cuddle buddies, sharing a cosy spot by the window. These moments remind us that even amid power struggles and territory disputes, our furry companions always have room for love, friendship, and mutual respect.

As cat owners, it's important to understand and respect the social hierarchy that naturally emerges among our pets. By observing their behaviour and body language, we can gain valuable insights into their relationships and help foster a harmonious living environment for all. Cats communicate through subtle cues:

- **Tail Flick**: Indicates agitation; step back and give the cat space.

- **Slow Blink**: A sign of trust; slowly blink back to build a stronger bond.

- **Headbutt**: A gesture of affection and ownership.

- **Purring**: Often a sign of contentment, but it can also be a self-soothing behaviour in times of stress.

- **Ears Back**: A clear sign that the cat feels threatened or uncomfortable.

Learning to interpret these signals can help us better support their interactions. These practical actions can foster better relationships among the cats and ensure a more harmonious household. Plus, it's just plain fun to sit back and watch the show unfold, like a never-ending sitcom starring our favourite feline characters. The drama, the comedy, and the unexpected plot twists make every day an adventure.

One key to a happy multi-cat home is ensuring each cat feels secure in their role within the household. This may involve providing distinct resources for each cat, such as separate feeding areas or multiple high perches for those who love to survey their domain. Cats thrive in an environment where their needs are met without competition or stress, and it's up to us to create that environment.

So next time you catch your cats engaging in a heated stare-down over a favourite sleeping spot or playfully chasing each other through the house, take a moment to appreciate the joy of cat-archy. Embrace the humour and beauty of their social dynamics, and remember that while cats may rule the roost, we are the lucky ones who get to share our homes with these fascinating creatures.

After all, who needs reality TV when you have a house full of cats? Their antics, expressions, and interactions provide endless entertainment, reminding us of the joy of living with such independent yet loving companions.

Cats also teach us valuable lessons about resilience, independence, and love. Their ability to adapt to changing dynamics within the household, find their niche, and establish meaningful connections with each other is truly remarkable.

Observing your cats, you may notice that their relationships can shift—one cat may take on a more dominant role as another age, or a previously aloof cat may become more sociable over time. These shifting roles and relationships highlight the fluid nature of feline social structures and remind us that flexibility is key to cohabitating peacefully.

Your Cat's Rank at Home: Embracing the Quirks and Personalities of Your Feline Family

Have you ever wondered where your cat stands in the social hierarchy of your household? It may surprise you to learn that your feline friend may be more of a boss than you think! Cats have their own unique personalities and quirks that dictate their rank at home, and it's important to embrace and understand these traits to maintain a harmonious relationship with your furry family member.

First and foremost, it's essential to recognize that cats are natural-born leaders. They may not be the ones paying the bills or doing the grocery shopping, but in their minds, they are the rulers of the roost. From their confident posture to demanding meows, cats exude an air of authority that is hard to ignore.

- **Regal Posture**: Cats sit tall with a proud demeanour.

- **Demanding Meows**: Their vocal commands testify to their instinctual desire to lead.

- **Territory Claiming**: Confidently claiming their favourite spots.

- **Patrolling Behavior**: Regularly walking through the home to ensure everything is in order.

- **Strategic Napping**: Choosing spots that offer a vantage point, demonstrating their watchful oversight.

So next time your cat gives you that demanding look, remember who's in charge! Their confidence and ability to command your attention testify to their instinctual desire to lead.

Each cat's unique personality shapes its rank within the household:

- **Social Butterflies**: Constantly seeking attention and affection. These cats often assert themselves as the top cat, demanding the best napping spots and first dibs on treats.

- **Introverted Cats**: Prefer to observe from the sidelines quietly. Their calming presence can help maintain balance within the group, diffusing potential conflicts before they escalate.

- ◦ **Example**: An introverted cat might help de-escalate a tense situation by calmly sitting nearby, showing the more dominant cats that there is no immediate threat.

- **Playful Instigators**: These cats enjoy stirring things up, often initiating playful chases or wrestling matches. They help keep the household lively and encourage social interaction among the other cats.

- **Peacekeepers**: Cats who step in when tensions rise, using calm body language or gentle nudges to diffuse conflicts.

It's important to remember that just like people, cats have their own individual preferences and boundaries. Some cats may be perfectly content to share their space with other pets, while others may prefer to be the sole ruler of the household. Understanding and respecting your cat's unique personality can help create a peaceful and harmonious living environment for you and your feline family members.

- **Provide Spaces for Retreat**: Allow each cat to have a designated area for alone time.

- **Create Opportunities for Social Interaction**: Encourage play when they are in the mood.

- **Understand Preferences**: Prevent conflicts by respecting each cat's boundaries.

- **Offer Vertical Territory**: Cat trees and shelves allow cats to establish their own space without competing for ground-level territory.

- **Individual Feeding Stations**: Ensure that each cat has a separate feeding area to reduce competition and stress.

Understanding these nuances helps prevent conflicts and ensures that each cat feels secure in their place within the household.

In the grand scheme of things, your cat's rank at home may seem trivial. But to your furry friend, it's a matter of pride and prestige.

By embracing and celebrating your cat's quirks and personalities, you can strengthen the bond between you and your feline family members, creating a happy and harmonious home for all. So next time your cat struts around like they own the place, just remember—they probably do! And that's okay because their confidence and unique personality are what make them such delightful companions.

Embracing these traits allows you to appreciate each cat's individuality, making your home a more enriching and joyful place for everyone.

The Claws and Order Way: Establishing Harmony and Balance in Your Multi-Cat Household

Welcome to our Claws and Order Way, where we strive to establish harmony and balance in your multi-cat household. As any cat owner knows, managing a group of feline furballs can be tricky. But fear not; with a little understanding of your cat's social hierarchy, you can create a peaceful coexistence among your beloved pets.

First and foremost, it's important to recognize that cats are natural-born rulers. They have a keen sense of hierarchy and will establish their own pecking order within your household. This means that you may have one cat who reigns supreme while others fall in line accordingly. It's all about finding that delicate balance of power and respect among your furry companions.

- **Balance Can Shift Over Time**: Cats age, new cats are introduced, or relationships change.

- **Signs of Shifts**: Increased aggression, avoidance, changes in sleeping or eating habits.

- **Supporting Changing Dynamics**:

  - Provide additional resources.

  - Adjust routines.

○ Offer individual attention to reduce tension.

To maintain peace in your multi-cat household, it's crucial to establish rules and boundaries early on. Cats thrive on routine and structure, so setting clear expectations for behaviour will help prevent any power struggles or conflicts. Whether it's designated feeding times, separate sleeping areas, or designated play spaces, creating a structured environment will help your cats understand their place in the hierarchy.

- **Routine Reduces Stress**: Establish feeding schedules and playtimes.

- **Structured Environment**: Designate feeding times and sleeping areas to reduce power struggles.

    ○ **Example**: Feeding your cats simultaneously in separate locations can prevent food-related aggression and ensure everyone gets their fair share without conflict.

- **Designated Play Spaces**: Create areas specifically for play to help channel energy positively and reduce competition for shared spaces.

In addition to setting boundaries, providing plenty of resources for your cats to avoid territorial disputes is important.

- **Multiple Resources**: Have multiple litter boxes, scratching posts, and feeding stations to prevent competition.

    ○ **Rule of Thumb**: One more litter box than the number of cats.

    ○ **Vertical Spaces**: Cat trees, shelves, and window perches help cats claim their own territory.

- **Safe Zones**: Create quiet areas where more introverted cats can retreat when they need space away from the action.

Creating a peaceful multi-cat household also involves understanding the signals your cats give each other.

- **Signs Cats Need Space:**

    ○ Hissing, growling, or swatting.

    ○ Ears flattened back, tail puffed up.

- **Respect Cues**: Redirect attention with toys like wand toys or laser pointers.

- **Reinforce Positive Interactions**: Treats like catnip-flavored biscuits can help diffuse tense situations.

Remember, your role as the mediator is to provide support without forcing interactions that could lead to stress or conflict. Creating an environment where each cat feels safe and valued is key to maintaining harmony.

A little humour goes a long way when managing a multi-cat household. Embrace the chaos and quirks of your feline friends, and enjoy the humour in their antics. Whether it's a cat asserting dominance over a cardboard box or two cats competing for the sunniest spot, these moments make life with cats amusing and delightful. Understanding your cat's social hierarchy and adopting the Claws and Order Way can foster a peaceful and balanced environment for your furry companions to thrive.

Each cat in your home brings something unique to the social dynamic, and their relationships will change over time. Be attentive to these shifts, and always be ready to offer support, whether through providing extra space, adjusting routines, or simply offering a comforting presence.

Final Words of Wisdom for Multi-Cat Households

Living with multiple cats can be challenging and rewarding. The key to a harmonious household is understanding that every cat has its own role and that these roles can evolve.

- **Be Patient**: Cats need time to adapt to each other and find their place.

- **Provide Plenty of Resources**: Multiple feeding stations, litter boxes, and perches can reduce competition.

- **Enjoy the Quirks**: Don't forget to laugh at the everyday antics of your feline friends.

Cherish the moments of peaceful grooming sessions, the playful chases, and even the dramatic standoffs. Embrace the uniqueness of each cat's personality, and remember that building a peaceful multi-cat home is a journey filled with humour, love, and learning. After all, our cats may rule the household, but we are fortunate enough to share in their wonderful, unpredictable world.

Cats remind us of the importance of independence and the beauty of companionship. They are creatures of habit but also masters of adaptability. With patience, observation, and much love, your multi-cat household can become a harmonious haven. So, when the drama unfolds, sit back, enjoy the show, and remember—you're living in the best kind of reality series starring your favourite feline friends.